Brief NLP Therapy

Brief Therapies Series

Series Editor: Stephen Palmer
Associate Editor: Gladeana McMahon

Focusing on brief and time-limited therapies, this series of books is aimed at students, beginning and experienced counsellors, therapists and other members of the helping professions who need to know more about working with the specific skills, theories and practices involved in this demanding but vital area of their work.

Books in the series:

Solution-Focused Therapy
Bill O'Connell

*A Psychodynamic Approach to Brief
Counselling and Pyschotherapy*
Gertrud Mander

Brief Cognitive Behaviour Therapy
Berni Curwen, Stephen Palmer and Peter Ruddell

Solution-Focused Groupwork
John Sharry

Transactional Analysis Approaches to Brief Therapy
Keith Tudor

Brief NLP Therapy

Ian McDermott
and
Wendy Jago

SAGE Publications
London • Thousand Oaks • New Delhi

First published 2001

 SAGE Publications Ltd
6 Bonhill Street
London EC2A 4PU

SAGE Publications Inc
2455 Teller Road
Thousand Oaks, California 91320

SAGE Publications India Pvt Ltd
32, M-Block Market
Greater Kailash – I
New Delhi 110 048

British Library Cataloguing in Publication data

A catalogue record for this book is available from the British Library

ISBN 0 7619 5965 3
ISBN 0 7619 5966 1 (pbk)

Library of Congress Control Number available

Typeset by Mayhew Typesetting, Rhayader, Powys
Printed in Great Britain by Biddles Ltd, Guildford, Surrey

For Ed Reese LCSW and MaryAnn Reese LMFT,
who were outstanding clinicians long before they
became exceptional NLP trainers.

Contents

About the Authors

Ian McDermott is a United Kingdom Council of Psychotherapy (UKCP) accredited psychotherapist who has been working with clients since 1980 and actively using NLP in clinical practice since 1984. Having trained in a variety of approaches ranging from Gestalt, to Bioenergetics, to Group Analysis, he considers NLP to be an invaluable unifying model of successful therapeutic intervention.

A leading trainer, consultant and author in the field of NLP and systems thinking and a Certified Trainer of NLP, he was made an International NLP Diplomate in 1994 in recognition of his contribution to the field.

As Director of Training for International Teaching Seminars he has been responsible for developing, supervising and in part delivering major 20-day NLP certification trainings at all levels. These include Practitioner, Master Practitioner and post-graduate programmes such as the Health Certification Training. His primary focus recently has been developing a full-scale Coaching Certification Programme which integrates NLP and coaching.

He has authored numerous NLP tape sets including *An Introduction to NLP: Psychological Skills for Understanding and Influencing People* (Thorsons, 1996), *NLP: Health and Well-Being* (Thorsons, 1996), both with Joseph O'Connor, as well as *Freedom from the Past* (ITS Audio, 1995), *Tools for Transformation* (ITS Audio, 1996) and distance learning packs such as *The Professional Development Programme* (ITS Audio, 1997). His work on creativity has been videoed by the BBC and is now part of the Open University's MBA Programme.

A regular contributor to television, radio and the national press, his books have been translated into 15 languages. They include: *Principles of NLP* (Thorsons, 1996), *NLP and Health* (Thorsons, 1996), *Practical NLP for Managers* (Gower, 1997), *The Art of Systems Thinking* (Thorsons, 1997), all with Joseph O'Connor, *Develop Your Leadership Qualities* (Time-Life, 1995), *Take Control of Your Life* (Time-Life, 1996) (with Joseph O'Connor and others), *NLP and the New Manager* (Texere, 1998), *Manage Yourself, Manage Your Life* (Piatkus, 1999) (both with Ian Shircore), *NLP Coach* (Piatkus, 2001) (with Wendy Jago).

Ian McDermott can be contacted through www.itsnlp.com

Wendy Jago is a Master Practitioner in NLP and certified NLP Coach and has been in practice as a therapist, consultant and trainer since the early 1980s. Formerly a Lecturer in English and Senior Lecturer in Education at the Universities of Sussex and Brighton, she has also been extensively involved in the in-service training of varied professional groups including teachers, social workers, probation officers, health professionals and psychotherapists.

In helping people with a wide range of personal and professional issues, she draws upon NLP, Rogerian counselling and Ericksonian hypnotherapy, tailoring her approach to the needs of each client.

She is co-author with Jan Pye of *Effective Communication in Practice* (Churchill Livingstone, 1998), and is engaged in writing on a variety of applications of NLP in the fields of therapy, management and sports performance.

Introduction

I enjoy the discovering of order in experience. It seems inevitable that I seek for the meaning or the orderliness or lawfulness in any large body of experience. It is this kind of curiosity, which I find very satisfying to pursue, which has led me to each of the major formulations I have made . . . (Carl Rogers, *On Becoming a Person*, 1967: 24)

Neuro-Linguistic Programming grew from the study of excellence in communication, and continues to be inclusive in its recognition of excellence wherever found. So in outlining some of the salient features of NLP, we are also necessarily honouring good practice. For the same reason, though one could say there is 'an NLP way of working', many of its elements will be found in the offices and consulting rooms of practitioners working with different therapeutic backgrounds in a variety of contexts.

So what is special about the contribution that NLP makes to the practice of therapy, and, specifically, to brief therapy? First and foremost, since its methods have been derived from detailed studies of outstanding therapists it offers practitioners the opportunity to enhance their effectiveness. Extrapolated from excellent practice, NLP delivers practical tools that work and a way of thinking which gives both therapists and clients new ways of understanding and exploring how we create a world for ourselves which can be heaven or hell. Just as its therapeutic repertoire is based on commonalities – values, presuppositions, communication and change skills – shared by very different approaches, so it can be used effectively by practitioners from a variety of schools.

NLP asks the question 'How do they do that?' – not just about the skilled practitioners its founders studied, but also about the way human beings structure their experience and make meaning of their worlds. It is this curiosity, with its concomitant excitement, which Rogers described as being part of his experience. It goes hand in hand with a respectful attentiveness to the experience of clients seeking help – and to the ways these clients structure the parts of their lives in which they function easily and well. It continues to exercise our developing awareness of how we too structure our maps of 'reality'; and it makes the experience of working with NLP a personal, as well as professional, adventure.

In keeping with this, we decided to write a book which aims to explore some of the key features of brief therapeutic change work with NLP. The first part is concerned with processes: the nature of therapeutic change; the significance of the presuppositions which client and therapist each bring to the work; the core process of modelling, which has always been at the heart of NLP; the inter-connected workings of the mind–body system and its implications for therapy. The second part is concerned with the people involved: what implications are there if we consider the client–therapist rela-tionship as a system, in which any input by one or other will inevitably affect the system as a whole? As might be expected, we look at the benefits to the client of NLP brief therapy. More challengingly, we consider the benefits to the therapist, for it is our belief that therapists can, and should, benefit too. The third part offers an account of one six-session case and a transcript of a single-session case. The longer case combines an account of the sessions together with a commentary on the therapy's development from an NLP viewpoint. The transcript of the shorter case is given without commentary in order to demonstrate the multi-levelled flow of the work. We have placed these examples at the end of the book so that, having already gained an understanding of how NLP works as a brief therapy, you will find them a richer illustration of the range of processes involved.

The book is thus an exploration of practicalities, and in keeping with this approach we have illustrated each chapter with a rich range of case-examples, which illustrate not only that NLP works, but how it worked specifically for particular clients with particular issues. To assist further practical application, we have offered at the end of each chapter in the first section three kinds of working NLP tools. There is, first, a *Conceptual Model*; second, exercises for practitioners and for supervisors, which we have called *Skill-builders*; and, third, a specific NLP change intervention which we have labelled a *Trans-former*, which has already proven its structural robustness and efficacy and can be readily incorporated into your existing thera-peutic repertoire.

We have also added at the end of the book information about books and training (Resources and Training) if you want to explore further.

The first question to ask about any therapeutic approach is: 'Does it work?' And the second question is 'How does it work?' Whenever you ask these questions with curiosity you are engaging in a spirit of open yet rigorous enquiry that is the very essence of NLP.

These were the questions we asked of NLP when we first encountered it. Should you choose to be even half as curious as we were, we believe you will find your time well spent in reaching your own conclusions.

Part 1:
Working with NLP: A Distinctive Orientation

1
Change

Meanings are not determined by situations, but we determine
ourselves by the meanings we give to situations.
(Alfred Adler, *The Individual Psychology of Alfred Adler*, 1964)

A book about brief therapy is a book about change. Change is what the
client wants and what the therapist expects to facilitate. The contract,
whether implicit or explicit, is that as a result of their work together,
something will be different. The client will feel, or think, differently in
some way; the client will be able to act differently. Whether the frame
relates to the client's past, their management of the present or their
hopes and intentions for the future, the agenda is to make a difference.

In introducing NLP as a form of brief therapy, we want to explore with
you some of the ways in which NLP goes about working with this
agenda. This book is part of a series on different forms of brief therapy,
which helps us to make an important point at the outset: good therapy
wears many hats, and at its root is the respectful mutuality of the
relationship between therapist and client, whatever the discipline. NLP
was based on the detailed and painstaking observation of outstanding
therapists from different fields, an observation which led to the discovery that despite their differences there were some key patterns of
skills, attitudes and strategies they held in common. NLP, as a working
tool for improving human relations, with wide-ranging applications in
personal therapy, education, creativity and business, is based on those
patterns. We hope, and believe, that in reading this book you will find
aspects of yourself and your work with others, perhaps differently
described but recognisable nonetheless, as well as encountering concepts, skills and strategies that are less familiar but extraordinarily useful.

Change, beliefs and identity

Where does the client start? Usually, with an idea that something is
not right. Sometimes this may be very specific – 'I want to stop doing
something' (smoking, hitting my wife, saying yes when I mean no) –
sometimes very vague – 'I just don't feel right, I should be happy but
I'm not'. Implicit in coming for help is that the change which is
needed is one which moves away from this uncomfortable situation,

this unpleasant or undesired behaviour. If the client no longer feels, or behaves, like this they will be satisfied.

There is an interesting issue here. How would the client know if they were 'better'? Answer: if they *did not* do/feel/think something any more. Sometimes a client will even go so far as to say they would like things to be as if *x* had never happened. The problem is easier to pinpoint if we translate the situation into another field. How do we know if we are well? Not, surely, by checking that we are *not ill*. We have an internal blueprint of wellness which is not negatively defined, even if sometimes it is experienced as neutral rather than actively positive. More often, though, we sense our wellness in clear experiential terms: energy, interest, enthusiasm, easy free movement, clear thought processes, good sleep and appetite, *joie de vivre*.

In contrast to such positives, framing a therapeutic goal as the absence of a distressing feature is both unambitious and self-limiting. It defines the solution in terms of the problem. A hypnotherapist would point out that since the unconscious cannot process statements which are grammatically negative without first calling up the item which is not wanted, negatively framed goals may well act at an unconscious level to perpetuate the problem. The principle is an important one and obvious once you see it in action. Try this instruction: *Do not think of a blue tree*. Notice how in order to follow the instruction you have to invoke that which you seek to negate.

While the client's beliefs about therapy are often that its purpose will be achieved if something ceases, the NLP therapist's beliefs are significantly different. NLP is much more ambitious, and a frequent opening question to the client may well be a version of 'What do you want?' Where the initial response is one of moving away from the undesired, the therapist may ask the client to imagine how life will be different once the undesired is no longer happening, and what other effects might ensue. Whether implicitly or explicitly, the goal has been enlarged, to encompass the discovery of what James Paul Gustafson called 'large, benign effects on other fields of the patient's life' (in Zeig and Gilligan, 1990, p. 409).

An example from one of our cases will illustrate both the process and the way in which the therapist may facilitate it. A young woman had explained in her initial telephone call that she had difficulties in her relationship with her mother. After greeting her on her arrival for the first appointment, the therapist began the session by reminding her of their brief discussion:

> T: You said on the phone that you wanted some help in your relationship with your mother . . .
> C: Yes, I don't want to be so caught up in it!
> T: Caught up . . .?

C: Preoccupied by it, over-reacting to it, worrying about it.
T: And if you weren't . . .?
C: Then I'd be able to relate to her normally.
T: And what would that mean for you?
C: Well, I wouldn't dread her phonecalls. I could enjoy talking with her about everyday things instead of getting so irritated at how trivial it all is. I wouldn't feel so angry and defensive when she makes any kind of criticism.
T: So how would you be instead . . .?
C: Oh – I'd be able to take what she says on board – or not! – or just think it's her way of feeling in control.
T: And if you were able to take it like that . . .?
C: I'd feel more independent – more grown-up.

A series of open-ended questions by the therapist prompt the client to make a shift from what she doesn't want to what she does, and at the same time from concerns at a level of behaviour, to underlying issues at a much more significant level – that of her identity. (The NLP model of Logical Levels which elucidates these distinctions is explored further in the Conceptual Model section of this chapter.)

Change, in other words, is seen as systemic rather than discrete. To take an example from our own experience, a client who is able to overcome her fear of flying and her anxiety about driving becomes more confident and assertive and moves towards realising her previously very tentative ambition to become more than 'just a doctor's receptionist'. An adult client who is able to change his internal experience of being criticised as a child by a hostile teacher finds that much of his blocked-off learning can now be more freely applied in the varied arenas of his life.

If change is systemic, its effects can be wide-ranging. This is something we know instinctively: intuited consequences of our desired change may enhance, or block, our progress. A very overweight client had managed to lose a stone relatively easily, then plateaued out by resuming some of her old eating patterns. Asked about the thinner self she envisaged in her future, she expressed anxiety about becoming 'thin and snappy' like a work colleague, and more indirectly wondered what would happen to her close relationship with her father if she found a boyfriend or husband. Literally, she was wondering if this thinner person could be 'her'.

Our identity is at the core of our concern, and beliefs about how it may be affected by therapeutic change are of crucial importance for client and therapist in their work together. In terms of NLP, the therapist is able to view the client's desired areas of change at different levels of specificity. At one extreme, the client can be assisted to make the desired changes more achievable by identifying them in clear and specific detail. On the other hand taking a wider, more systemic, meta-level view of the effects such a change may have on their life, their relationships, their work and their ambitions will help obviate any blocking coming from a need to avoid unconsciously perceived disadvantages.

It is one thing for the therapist to feel comfortable about the relationship between identity and change, and sometimes quite another for the client to do so. Carl Rogers (1967) described how the client's progress in therapy is one of increasing flexibility and fluidity: 'He has changed, but what seems most significant, he has become an integrated process of changingness' (p. 158). Rogers perceives no inherent contradiction between personal evolutionary process and a sense of recognisable self. What of the client, however, who wants to feel different, behave differently, while explicitly stating 'People don't change'?

NLP has important resources to offer the therapist at this point. One is *rapport*, one of the crucial cornerstones of any effective communication. The client's statement comes over as one of belief, but it's unlikely to be helpful to attempt to argue rationally with it – unless this particular client is so rooted in rationality that they are really wanting the therapist to offer evidence that incontrovertably proves that people *do* change. Rapport involves, among other things, meeting the client in their own frame of reference, and it may well be that this client will find it easier to accept an agreement that people don't *fundamentally* change, but that they can *modify their behaviour*. Implicit here is a second key concept: how we structure our experience is a matter of learning. What has been learnt can potentially be altered, refined, added to or recontextualised so as to shift the meaning it has for us in quite far-reaching ways. It can be reframed.

NLP is based on the observation of the effects of human learning at informal and unconscious levels, as well as formal and conscious ones. Body and brain have an astounding capacity to recognise, imitate and enact increasingly complex processes and sequences. Learning as such is neutral: it comes, as it were, with the package. (The effects of learning, as we all know, can be heavily loaded.) The corollary of this is threefold:

- What is learnt can be broken down into its component parts.
- What has been learnt can be taught (i.e. transferred from one person to another, from one context to another).
- What has been learnt can be relearnt (i.e. changed).

Therapeutic change is often truly miraculous; but the miracles are those of the human capacity to learn and relearn. A therapist–client contract based upon this supposition is at once more realistic, and more life-enhancing – for both. The process of such a redefinition –

this isn't about fundamental change but about different learning – is known within NLP as a 'reframe': it takes the statement presented by the client and by re-presenting it with a radically different emphasis opens up a way forward which had previously been closed off.

Within NLP, then, the therapist seeks to work with the client to bring about changes which not only alleviate the presenting problem but in so doing provide experiences and learnings from which the client can generate further life-enhancing experiences. The word 'learnings', though unfamiliar, is significant: derived from Milton Erickson, the original verbal form (-ing), hidden in the current use as a noun, draws our attention to the fact that learning is a process, and therefore carries the potential of further movement. It is not 'finished', a thing complete, as the word 'learnt' (or 'taught') so easily implies.

This particular attention to the detail of language is itself characteristic of good therapy, and especially of NLP. Its fine variations provide us not only with cues and clues but with economical, elegant, specifically targeted means of leverage. This is something we will return to later.

NLP, then, is a therapy of what is possible: it opens for client and therapist a voyage which is genuinely into the unknown. A fundamental assumption in NLP is that a client should always leave the therapist's room with more choices than they came in with. These choices result from therapeutic changes which open up the realm of possibility while at the same time respecting the client's original 'shopping list'. (This is the very opposite of the kind of procedure which by identifying or labelling a hitherto unremarked upon part of the client's pathology, 'gives' them a problem which they didn't 'have' before.)

A belief that change is generative, offering the client the chance to gain even more than they bargained for, is at the root of NLP. And there are other related beliefs within NLP which go even further in turning the received, or traditional, concepts of some therapy around as we shall see.

Many current notions of therapy in Western culture are largely derived from a filtering down of ideas about Freud and Freudian psychotherapy as practised by his followers. In this received mythology, therapy is seen as arduous, possibly painful, slow and often difficult. Even more recent brief therapies leave much of this assumed characterisation intact. Clients coming for therapy often reveal how they too have taken this cultural view for granted: 'I know it won't be easy . . .' 'I know things can't change overnight . . .' 'I'm not expecting miracles . . .' 'I'm prepared to go through whatever it takes'. Indicative phrases we've heard even among professionals include 'No pain, no gain'; 'if it doesn't hurt, it doesn't heal'.

While we would not deny that therapy may at times resemble these descriptions, it is our clinical experience, and our belief, that it is also exciting, fun, natural, joyful, playful, amusing and rapid. What is it that encourages the 'traditional', more laborious typology, and makes some people suspect this more light-hearted one? It may be that there is a vestige here of a protestant, even puritanical, equating of 'seriousness' in the sense of 'importance', with seriousness in the sense of 'absence of joy'. Therapists and therapies can at times be very dour: depression in the client can be matched by a heaviness in the therapist; sadness by a joyless intensity. The intention may be to convey respect, but the effect may be a reinforcement of the problem.

Again, it helps to look at the analogy of 'natural' learning. Wendy still remembers the delight of being able to say the alphabet aloud for the first time: it hadn't been 'hard work' to learn it – in fact, the realisation was more that all of a sudden the completed list was 'just there'. In much the same vein, an elderly client turned to her while leaving the house after a particularly emotional session and said: 'This is so exciting, you know!' Both experiences were ones in which there was a sense of things coming together.

All beliefs have consequences. If you believe that therapy is strenuous and frequently painful, those assumptions include the probability that the client will at times find it uncomfortable and hard. And when people find things hard and uncomfortable, they frequently 'resist', even while overtly acknowledging that the process will in the long run be 'good for them'. The larger (meta) concept includes the smaller. Conversely, when clients 'work at' their therapy, both they and their therapist may well be pleased that they are 'making progress'.

Contrast this with the kind of effort that is involved in achieving something we are really impelled to do: a teenager who learns every detail about his football club's performance, not only present but past, and from there enlarges his expertise to include other clubs past and present; or a baby determined to crawl, or to stand and walk. Learning has built-in imperatives; and the learner may well discount, or even be unaware of, the considerable mental or physical effort involved. How many parents encourage a would-be toddler by reminding him or her that learning to walk is difficult, time-consuming, sometimes painful but worth the effort in the end?

What happens, on the other hand, if you presume that emotional and mental health are as much part of the human blueprint as physical health, and that the organism has similarly built-in drives to maintain, or return to, that blueprint? Effort will at times be required, certainly – but an effort similar to that of the immune system focusing its astoundingly precise resources to maintain or restore health: an effort which is appropriately and instinctively targeted through innate self-monitoring (often largely unconscious); an effort designed for precisely that function. There will be an inner certitude that the effort is rightly directed, with the potential to improve the situation significantly. There will usually be an ability to search out appropriate resources, internal or external. There will be an equally finely monitored sensitivity to degrees of improvement.

Teenagers often comment on their awareness – almost a physical perception – that their minds and emotions are growing. It is as though the rapidity of the changes which they are undergoing at many levels brings itself to startling consciousness. It is our experience that as clients find resources to heal, restore and enrich their lives they also have a palpable sense of growth, energy and excitement at being themselves.

The necessary conditions for change

As long ago as the 1960s, the American psychologist Abraham Maslow described the essential paradox of change (*Toward a Psychology of Being*, pp. 46–47). Once their fundamental survival needs have been met, he argued, human beings oscillate between two essential, polarised needs: the need for *safety* and the need for *growth*. A sufficient amount of either prods the person in the direction of the other. Too much safety becomes boring – seek what will make you grow. Too much growth feels dangerous – seek safety. This simple paradigm is immensely useful to the therapist – and enabling once explained to the client. The implications for the therapeutic context are clear: meet the client's needs for safety, and they will inevitably seek out opportunities for growth. This is a radically different kind of drive from the one many clients will have first arrived with – the need to get *away from* (a situation, a behaviour, a problem, a relationship, a phobic response, their past history) – and it is a fundamental and exciting part of working as partners using NLP.

Sensitivity to this oscillation can enable therapist and client to monitor quite precisely the appropriateness of what is going on, as it is going on. For example, a client who in his first session had spent very substantial amounts of time in unprompted inner reflection as he considered why he had come, how his childhood experience had contributed to his present difficulties, and what he might possibly hope for in the future, said in his second session that he felt 'more in the front of my head than last time', and that this (more cognitive, conversational) kind of interaction was what he needed at this point.

We would consider his inward-looking reflection, with its concomitant physical stillness, smoothed muscle tone and unfocused eyes, an example of a naturalistic trance state. When we are deeply absorbed in thought, perhaps searching our memories, going over experiences, imagining future scenarios or seeking solutions, we automatically make alterations in our physio-psychological state, which closely resemble those occurring in formal trance states. We all know how to go into a trance, we just don't always recognise that this is what is happening, or give it that label. In describing how his subjective experience differed from one session to another, this client recognised that it was different experientially. He needed to engage in different kinds of processing on the two occasions; and his therapist's attentiveness to the details of the client's ongoing behaviour meant that they both knew what he was talking about.

Maslow's typology suggests the oscillation between safety and growth is inbuilt and natural. Client and therapist can respond to it, use it and sometimes jointly decide to give it a helping hand. There is no need for client and therapist to have separate agendas: as in the therapist thinking they know where the client 'needs to go' and using their considerable expertise to influence that movement. People move because they want to: in the view of NLP this is a natural, inbuilt process. If experience has blocked it or channelled it in unfruitful ways, the process is so fundamental that, like a seed in dry ground, it is usually only waiting for some very specific condition to be met (moisture, warmth, seasonal change, fire) in order to restart. Where the therapist can provide a *safe environment together with the excitement of potential change*, the neccesary conditions for growth are met.

The metaphor is one of facilitating natural growth, the belief that human beings have the capacity for life-long learning. Our ability to reflect upon experience means that we will inevitably learn something from our experience, for good or ill. One view of the therapist's role within NLP is that the therapist provides the context for learning/relearning, a context which is mediated through interaction with the client.

What kinds of interaction facilitate the client in this process? From observing outstanding therapists, the NLP model identifies two crucial and related processes: 'pacing' and 'leading'. 'Pacing' means just that – going at the client's pace. Learning to do this is fundamental to NLP. At its simplest this means taking the trouble to get in sync with the client by adopting a similar kind of posture; talking at a similar rate in a similar pitch; breathing at a comparable rate; it might mean using similar kinds of language – both words and metaphors. The importance of this simple behavioural pacing becomes very clear if we imagine its opposite: a client who is contemplative encountering a therapist who is highly energetic, talking fast and making lots of gestures; or a client who is lively and bouncy while their therapist is staid, physically contained, verbally minimalist. The contrast may leave the client feeling unheard, wrong, stupid or angry. The effect of respectful pacing (which is very different from mimicry) is to let the client know *outside of conscious awareness* that they are accepted and that their experience is valid.

Pacing may also have conscious components, of course, as we become aware when we sometimes fail to pace adequately by moving on too rapidly from problem/symptom/feelings and find the client bringing us back again. This is an example of how much pacing may be needed before we can fulfil our other function, which is to 'lead'.

The client may well value our ability to empathise with their situation, but they have come hoping to change it. They have sought outside help precisely because they cannot, at this time, find a way to change things themselves. The therapist provides, sometimes by example, sometimes cognitively, sometimes by specific procedures, the lead which the client needs to move forward. Leading without first pacing is not congruent to the client, and will probably either not be 'heard' or, if heard, may be rejected. Wendy remembers as a young university tutor spending some hours trying to help a troubled student, offering reassurance and cogent reasons designed to ameliorate his perception of his situation, only to be humbled by the truth of his rejecting statement: 'well, that's all just words, isn't it'. No pace, no lead.

Nonetheless, the client often comes with a stuckness, and the stuckness needs to be destabilised. Erickson (Rosen, 1982, pp. 251–2) often worked to destabilise a client's stuckness from within their existing framework of beliefs and values: a client who believed that she offended God by farting in church was at a crucial point in the therapy accused of insulting her Maker. When she protested, she was then given a long exposition on the wondrous ability of the anal sphincter to distinguish between liquids, solids and gases and to deal with each appropriately. Erickson paced her beliefs, then destabilised her intransigent and self-punitive application of them.

Another way to describe this process has been offered by the formative NLP writer and trainer Robert Dilts (1990) in *Changing Belief Systems with NLP*. There he shows how the structure of a problem is often made up in a molecular way, with different elements relating to each other in an apparently inevitable and interlocked way. By separating out the elements using one of the many NLP techniques that have been developed, the therapist frees the client from the felt permanence of the situation. To put it another way, the client has come with a certitude and is helped towards an enabling uncertainty. Certainty is the inhibitor of change, uncertainty is its seed-bed.

Leverage for change

NLP is a very practical therapy: it is driven by a curiosity expressed in the question 'how do you *do* that?' Initially, the focus was on the helper: *how* do these excellent communicators – Perls, Erickson, Satir – do what they do? The scope of the question widened: *how* do people actually structure their experience – both internally and externally? And this then leads to how does *this* client structure their problem experience (i.e. *how* do they do their problem?) , which leads on to the possibilities inherent in *how* does the therapist help them do it differently? The working assumption here is that knowing how something is done gives enormous leverage. Once we know how excellence is done, we have at our disposal the potential structures for excellence. Once we know how a problem is done, we have access to its structure, and can change it.

A client who had come for help with losing weight described how he would often binge at the end of the working day.

T: How do you actually go about that – bingeing, I mean? You say it's after work. So there you are, driving home . . . What happens?

C: I'll be driving home from work, and I'll somehow take a route that goes past Sainsbury's. I've already got food for supper in the fridge – stuff that fits in with my diet, but I drive in anyway. And I buy packs of sausage rolls and donuts and crisps, and then I go home and eat them.

T: Immediately? Or do you do anything else first? Do you add them to your supper, or what? I'm trying to get an idea . . . What would I see if I were there?

C: Nothing! I wouldn't do it if you were there!

T: Right! So you only do this on your own – but tell me, anyway, how you go about it. Everyone is different, and we need to know exactly how *you* go about it.

C: I feel very strange describing it – it's almost as if I'm watching myself . . . But ok. Well, let's see . . . I put my briefcase down and take my jacket off . . . Then I sit down in the kitchen and eat straight out of the packets. It's not a meal, so no plate – and I have to eat the crisps first, then the sausage rolls, then the donuts – all of them . . . Funny how rigid it sounds, now that I'm talking about it.

T: And what are you thinking about . . .?

C: Nothing, really, it's quite automatic, sort of mindless . . .

T: And are you enjoying the food?

C: I suppose I must be, at least to start with, but I'm not really noticing how it tastes.

By asking the client to be really detailed and specific about how he does his problem behaviour, the therapist elicits a range of important information, including:

- the scope and amount of the overeating;
- the ritualistic pattern involved;
- the degree of the client's dissociation;
- the automatic nature of the behaviour.

Any of these may provide not merely information but very specific targets for leverage in helping this particular client to achieve the changes he desires.

There is an important connection between change and learning. The brain learns fast – in conditions which load learning. The need for safety loads learning, as the rapid installation of phobias illustrates only too clearly – frequently we do not need a painful stimulus to be repeated in order to learn to avoid it, as the common phrase 'once bitten, twice shy' clearly expresses. The inbuilt human drive towards growth also loads learning: children learn what is natural and exciting to them, even if it is complex or apparently difficult; plants like bamboo and amaryllis make the most of their natural environmental conditions with astonishingly rapid growth; and the same inbuilt impulse towards healthy functioning, we believe, helps clients learn and relearn what they need to regain physical or emotional equilibrium. Timing, too, is critical – in the Erickson example we gave earlier, his intervention came after time spent pacing and preparing the client. The fact that the client has chosen to come for therapy may be another indicator of their internal readiness to change; one client said that she had carried a therapist's card in her wallet for two years before feeling that the time was right. In the same way, clients may talk about how they have found a self-help book incredibly helpful – 'Yet, you know, I've had it on my shelf for a long time, dipped into it and never got anywhere with it before.'

But if, as we have said, learning is systemic, then change also has system-wide implications. Like the ripple that pulses through the pond from a single stone, or the change in the colour of a liquid from the addition of dye, change spreads throughout the entire organism, reorganising and reconfiguring as it goes.

This has important implications. It means that what may on the surface appear like a 'mere' change in behaviour, can have cascading effects. A non-swimmer, terrified of water, who learns that water can be trusted and even enjoyed, is likely to approach other challenges with greater confidence – whether their fear was helped by an intensive swimming course, by systematic desensitisation or by hypnotic regression. The leverage has a systemic effect. An immobilising 'I can't' has been transformed into an ennabling 'Now I can', with implications that are likely to be far-reaching. Other problems may now be seen in a new frame – perhaps they too can be addressed and solved. Self-confidence will be enhanced, self-image improved. The aim in NLP is that the outcome can be more extensive than solving the problem, because the learning is available beyond the original context in which it was needed. For example, a client who had come for help in improving her self-confidence, especially in relation to her dominating mother, later reported that she had not only found ways to get some distance from her mother, but she had also begun to explore a different style in her creative work which felt 'more me', and had attended an assertiveness course.

This casts an interesting light on leverage. Potentially, any change can have systemic effects. The client's presenting problem is clearly their desired focus for leverage – that is why they came. Changes anywhere in the system may affect the person as a whole, and frequently changes in apparently less central and significant areas will help destabilise the fixity of the central problem, preparing it indirectly. Further, change can be more far-reaching, more liberating, more life-enhancing than the client dared to hope.

Many of the means of leverage which NLP utilises are processes which destabilise what is stuck, and help the client reinterpret and reorganise the elements of the problem into different, neutral or more positive constellations. While this book is not an encyclopaedia, we would at least like to offer some pointers as to how this is done in NLP. So here are some of the means of leverage used in NLP (NLP terminology or technology is given in brackets). We can:

- reorganise existing patterns of learnt behaviour/feeling (e.g. by changing sequences and strategies);
- shift perspective (e.g. through personal position shifts, representational system changes, taking a meta position);
- become less involved, or more fully involved, in specific experiences (e.g. through association/dissociation, changing representational system and modifying sub-modalities);
- recognise and manage emotional/behavioural states;
- reclaim ideas and experiences that have been reified and are therefore felt to be fixed, factual, outside the client's ability to control, and re-establish them as active and therefore manageable processes (through denominalising);
- use a variety of linguistic and experiential means to scramble existing dysfunctional body–mind (neurological) codings of experience so that more enabling patterns can be established;

● reclassify items as part of larger, or smaller, categorisations in order to recontextualise their meaning (e.g. by chunking up or down).

The fabric of change work

What is therapy working on? Generally, the assumption is that it works on 'the problem'. In NLP we have found it useful to describe the process in broader terms. The client's problem is part of how they, as a unique individual, structure their subjective experience. Their unique genetic heritage has been tempered by the varied learnings of their life experience to produce their own characteristic ways of understanding and being in the world; their problem is a part of this complex, personally characteristic encoding. The term 'Neuro-Linguistic Programming' itself indicates some of the dimensions of this complexity. The neurological functioning of mental experience, the key dimension of language as a mediator and determinant of meaning, the significance of patterning, repeated sequences and purposeful intent in our internal as well as external behaviour – these are the keys to understanding and working with the way we structure our unique subjective experience, and interact with that of others.

The success of any model lies in its ability to encompass, reliably and predictably, an extensive range of information, extrapolating core features in such a way as to include what is generally understood (believed, experienced) and also to accommodate what is individual, varied, unique. Because NLP is concerned with how humans structure their experience, its characteristic *how do you do that* questioning focuses us on shared or common processes which result in individually characteristic patterns. Those patterns, as we shall argue further in the chapter on presuppositions, are not in themselves good or bad – though they may have consequences that could be described in such judgemental terms. The patterns are the result of life experience acting upon the inherent need and capacity of human beings to make sense of their world, attaching meaning, sequencing, prediction and consequence to it. That is what they, and we, are working *on* when we work together.

What are we working *with*? Essentially, the answer is much the same. We are working with a shared ability to observe and reorder the elements of these patterns – with awareness of both self and other as processors. Any two golfers discussing the finer points of technique or match-play may be doing the same. The discussion is process based; the assumption is that where learning is involved, learning can continue. Players who work with a mentor or coach can be helped to become the evaluator, trainer, modifier and appreciative audience of their own performance. Within such a collaborative context, the skills of acute observation, linguistic appropriateness and subtlety, inter-active sensitivity, goal or outcome focus, self-awareness and self-monitoring all play important parts – as they do in NLP. (Indeed, this is one reason why NLP has been successfully applied in perform-ance arts and sports.)

These skills belong to both parties equally: NLP is in many ways a 'brain-user's guide'. As we will explore later, NLP is charac-teristically egalitarian and 'transparent' in its approach, and much of its portfolio of understandings and skills can be readily taught to the client. More significantly still, the components of the problem are at one and the same time the components of the solution. The closer the attention therapist and client pay together to the very framing of the problem, the more able they are to pinpoint what, where and how therapeutic reorganisations can take place. (We shall look at this in more detail in some of the case examples.) It was an understanding of this intimate relationship between problem and solution, this degree of finesse and exactitude in making minimal but precisely targeted adjustments that helped restructure the client's experience, that the early developers of NLP observed in their original models of therapeutic excellence. From this stand-point, NLP is more like an explanation of the principles of the internal combustion engine than a specific manual for maintaining, say, a Saab.

Change and the outcome frame

One important way in which NLP often makes this approach clear is through a characteristic initial question. Not 'What is the problem?' but 'What do you want?' It will be clear from what we said at the beginning of this chapter that this immediately sets a *towards* rather than an *away-from* focus. A first response from a client, well-conditioned to a problem-focus, may remain within an away-from frame: 'I want to stop x . . . feel less y . . .' It is clear that in such a case, the beginning of the therapy is in helping the client construct an idea of what life might offer after x or y. One important consequence of this is that clients who have become intimately habituated to their problem, perhaps over a long period of time, begin to build a notion not only of the future they want, but of what life will be like without the problem to define it. One client put this very clearly when she said 'I'm afraid that if I get better I don't know who I'll be'. In this context, the outcome-oriented question becomes a means of pacing the client. You don't have to begin changing, is the implication, until you know what change you want. No need to leave home until you know the direction in which those first steps will be taking you. There is also the further implication that more than one kind of change is possible, and that the choice belongs to the client. This is far removed from the high paternalism implicit in phrases like 'The client needs to . . .'.

For some clients, the question is so unexpected, and its implications so important, that it immediately provokes a profound natural trance. The face softens, the eyes defocus, the body immobilises. There is silence. There may after a while be a slow and wondering response: 'I don't know.' 'And if you did know . . .?' responds the therapist, in an equally slow and speculative tone. More internal search results, or perhaps a surprisingly clear and rapid, 'Well, then I'd do such-and-such'. One explanation would be that the open form of the question provoked an internal search, accessing an answer known unconsciously but hitherto not available to conscious awareness. The question could not be answered consciously, and triggered a sufficiently altered state of awareness to access other levels of processing. Whatever the explanation, clinical experience frequently demonstrates that such a beginning can have immense value to the therapeutic partners at the outset of their work together. Here's why:

- It provokes an internal search.
- It aids the client in identifying a desired outcome.
- In doing so, it begins the destabilisation of the 'problem frame' by shifting attention.
- It implicitly informs the client that the therapy is in their service (i.e. it shifts the power base which they may have come expecting).
- It provides a foundation for further exploration and clarification (for example, of whether the goal is realistic and how they will be able to tell when it has been achieved).
- It ensures that therapist and client have a shared representation of the goal for their work.
- It helps keep them 'on track', and also helps them evaluate the relative usefulness of excursions off it.
- It gives them both a reference by which to measure progress during the therapy, and to recognise and mark achievement as it comes to completion.

In this chapter we have explored some of the assumptions within NLP about the relationship between therapy and change, and considered what kind of implications these have for the client and the therapist as they begin their work together. It is often said that change can happen on many levels, and we want to offer you a practical set of distinctions about these levels. As therapists we have found these extraordinarily useful diagnostically. They are known as Logical Levels.

Conceptual model: Logical Levels

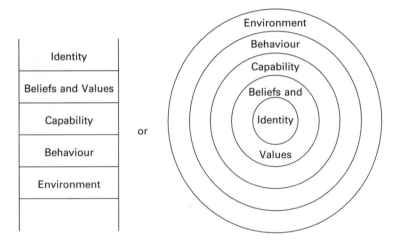

The model of the Logical Levels is one which helps us and our clients organise and place the information with which we are working. It tells us what kind of issue we are dealing with, and allows us to select appropriate means of addressing it. It was developed by Robert Dilts and Judith DeLozier (2000). As the above diagrams show, the levels can be thought of as either forming a hierarchy, ranging from the most external at the lowest level, to the most internal at the highest, or as a series of concentric circles, with the most personal and intimate at the centre and the least personal at the perimeter. Neither form is 'right': which you prefer to use depends on which suits you best and on the situation in which you are using it.

The chapter on change has been sequenced according to the Logical Levels model, and shows how change can be experienced, and facilitated, at any of the levels.

The hierarchy of the levels describes how we structure our experience on a continuum from most personal and internal (identity) to the most external (environment). In this model we cannot automatically assume that issues of Identity are more important than other issues, only that they are held as involving the self. Depending on the issue and the circumstances, we can be as significantly affected by concerns at other levels, either in themselves or because their impact is more extensive. For example, the long-working hours (environment) experienced in the UK by junior hospital doctors may have adverse effects upon their concentration (behaviour), their ability to draw quickly and accurately upon their skills (capability), erode their idealism (values) or even their sense of being a good doctor (identity).

Being able to identify the logical level of a problem we are working on, whether it is one-to-one, organisational, personal or client-related, enables us to be much crisper and more effective in the way we apply our understanding and our skills. Further, we can teach the model to our clients, thus enabling them in turn.

In terms of our clinical work, the logical levels model is also a valuable means of controlling possible automatic therapist-bias. It reminds us to check:

● at what level the issue or problem is being experienced by the client
● whether this is also the level at which the problem originates

and to explore at what level the most effective and elegant intervention might be made.

For example, a client who was an excellent and experienced manager but whose organisation was restructured, with concomitant changes to his job, came to feel that his skills were inadequate (capability). As a result, he began to lose faith in himself (identity). However, exploring the situation more fully revealed that the reformatted organisation emphasised significantly different priorities from the old (values). As a result of recognising the different levels involved, he regained faith in himself but recognised that he needed to look for a job in an organisation whose values were more congruent with his own (a change effected on the level of environment).

However, one of his colleagues had a quite different experience. He came to recognise that he needed additional training to cope with the changed demands (a change on the capability level). He felt that as long as he got that, he would fit right in.

In using the logical levels, we are reminded that the client's frame of reference is the essential starting point: this model is one which respects that, while offering ways to open up further understandings and wider choices.

For us as therapists, the benefits of this way of thinking are considerable. It alerts us to any bias we might have which would mean we would tend to focus on certain logical levels more than others because we're more comfortable or familiar with those domains, or because we assume they are more intrinsically significant. It also helps us gain greater flexibility in our clinical work. If we are willing to pay equal attention to information whatever the level, our skill at working across the levels increases. As we become more adept in this way, we also become more able to identify where an intervention or change at a lower level will bring about the desired change at higher levels. This is a very useful corrective to any therapeutic bias which assumes that clients' problems are 'really' or mostly ones of identity or beliefs.

Each of the logical levels is concerned with a particular class of issues, and helps us answer a specific kind of question:

- Identity – WHO?
- Beliefs and Values – WHY?
- Capability – HOW?
- Behaviour – WHAT?
- Environment – WHERE/WHEN?

We think there are two immediate considerations arising from this:

1) Whenever we ask one of these questions, we may be eliciting the class of information that it relates to. For example, if we ask a client 'why . . .' it will lead them into explanations, justifications and reasons, all of which rest upon beliefs and values.

2) We can train ourselves to notice whenever these words crop up in a client's speech. Again, they are signalling that specific kinds of issues are involved.

Equally, an awareness of the levels and their possible interrelationships may help us avoid inappropriate interventions and hear what our clients are really asking for. A doctor who had been attending a training Ian ran in Italy had been approached the day before by a patient with the words: 'Doctor, I feel very tense. I feel like I've forgotten how to relax.' Running the usual tests, the doctor rapidly concluded that the patient had high blood pressure, was indeed tense, and needed to address this. His intervention was to prescribe medication (a change at the level of behaviour) and to suggest that this patient take a break by going on vacation (a change of environment).

Reviewing the patient's words in the light of the logical levels, the doctor became aware that the patient had been telling him precisely what kind of intervention was needed. He didn't know *how* to relax – a capability. To achieve self-sustaining and permanent change he needed assistance at the level of capability – he needed to learn the skill of relaxing.

Conversely, another doctor was able to greatly enhance his bedside manner. He found that his patients relaxed more and were able to talk more fully and easily about their difficulties when he bought himself a reclining chair (environment) and ensured that he pushed it away from his desk to listen to them (behaviour). In bringing about a state change in himself in this way – comfort and increased informality made him more at ease – he was instrumental in bringing about a state change for the better in his patients too.

Change Skill-builders

Therapist
- Think about change as you experience it both personally and professionally, and jot down the structure of change experiences that were successful. How did you do that? What internal and external experiences, what deliberate acts or interventions, what conscious and what intuitive components, helped to bring about your successful changes?

Supervisor
- Ask your supervisee to identify the structure of a personally successful change experience, helping them to unpack the various components.

Logical Levels Skill-builders

Therapist
- With your next five clients, note the logical level at which you are working with the client primarily. Has this changed? If so, how?
- Take a recent problem you have worked on with a client and consider ways in which it could be approached on one or more of the *other* levels.
- Ask yourself, if you worked at a different level on this problem, would you achieve greater leverage?
- Ask yourself if you are particularly good at working at one or more of the levels (which?).

- Consider, do you have a bias against any of them as less therapeutically important?

Supervisor
Of every supervision session, ask yourself:

- Does this supervisee tend to present me with difficulties at a
  particular logical level in the case of a) a particular client or
  b) most of their clients?
- Does this supervisee have the skill and flexibility to engage with
  clients at all logical levels?
- Do I as a supervisor have the skill and flexibility to engage with
  my supervisees at all logical levels?

Change Transformer

'I can't do that'
Clients often say they 'can't do' something, and the word 'can't' has
a 'fact-like' quality which can easily go unchallenged. Yet it
effectively disguises a complex kind of generalisation. It implies that
the inability concerned is pervasive and permanent. It also skips over
any notion about important factors like cause and context.

NLP, with its emphasis upon curiosity and attentiveness, teaches
us to be curious about what is implied in our language use, just as
much as we are about what is made explicit. If we help the client to
fill in what is missing, we often help them obtain useful information.

In the case of 'can't', two approaches are particularly helpful:

1) *Client*: I can't do that.
   Therapist: What stops you?
2) *Client*: I can't do that.
   Therapist: What would happen if you did?

The effect of this first intervention is that it opens up information
about cause. We learn more about the inhibitory mechanism at
work. Either that, or the client may simply update themselves and
answer 'Well, nothing, actually.'

The second exposes anticipated consequences or effects, of which
the client may or may not be consciously aware. Again, it may also
trigger a realisation that nothing dire will happen. At times this is
sufficient for a client to feel empowered to do something different.

Both approaches shift the client from a position of powerlessness
to one in which they have a greater possibility of influence.

'I must do that'
Similar to 'I can't' in linguistic structure, this phrase, with its many everyday variations, also features largely in clients' language and experience. It too disguises important missing information, which can be filled in by a similar kind of questioning.

> *Client*: I must do that.
> *Therapist*: What would happen if you didn't?

Alternatively:

> *Client*: I mustn't do that.
> *Therapist*: What would happen if you did?

In both cases the question encourages the client to make explicit the hidden constraints which are operating, which in turn allows them to be considered and addressed at a variety of logical levels.

Every 'I can't' or 'I must' statement is a belief statement. It gives us privileged information about what this client believes is and is not possible for them given their map of the world. If we use the NLP questions we can gather more information about how this world hangs together. This is essential if we and the client are to expand the limits of their map of the world.

2

Presuppositions

A psychology that participates in the human enterprise must perceive that the guidelines chanelizing a person's processes are drawn by the person himself – that they are therefore personal constructs, and may be redrawn and revalidated by the user to structure anew his thought and behaviour. They are not the residue of biographical incidents, nor are they projected facsimiles of reality. They are, instead, the axes of reference man contrives to put his psychological space in order and to plot his various courses of action.

(George Kelly, *Clinical Psychology and Personality*, 1969).

Human interaction is not neutral: it is based on attitudes, beliefs, values and assumptions – in other words, on presuppositions. And in this, therapy is no exception. The therapist learns in training a more or less specialised set of 'therapeutic assumptions': about the therapy, about the role of the client, about their own role as change agent. They are also likely to spend appreciable amounts of time monitoring the possibilities of their own counter-transference, perhaps involving their own training therapy or ongoing supervision. Such processes are designed to safeguard the client, and the therapist.

It is the argument of NLP, however, that there are significant presuppositions around therapy which are very often unexamined, yet which crucially determine its context, its processes and therefore its possible outcomes.

As a prelude to outlining some of the underlying presuppositions which have been found useful within NLP, we'd like to tell you a story. A client who had previously been assessed by a psychiatrist reported that in her interview with him she had felt pressured to answer questions and that he had commented adversely on her 'refusal' to make eye-contact with him. He had also made it clear to her welfare officer at work that he found her reasons for seeking therapy vague to the point of being meaningless. The client had felt there was no rapport or even sympathy for her depression: the psychiatrist had told her she needed continuing psychiatric care and was reluctant to refer her, as she requested, for help with NLP. From the psychiatrist's letter to her doctor (copied to the NLP therapist) it was clear that this was an accurate account of his views.

The client attended her first NLP session with considerable trepidation, apologising for the fact that she found it difficult to be forthcoming about her traumatic experiences – she said that her welfare officer had had to 'drag information out of her' even though their relationship had been a good one. She was reassured that it was for her to decide how much detail she gave – the therapist believed that 'once is enough' and did not wish her to be retraumatised. She was asked what her aim was in seeking therapy, and immediately answered that she wished to build more self-confidence so that she would have a better base from which to sort out the past and manage her continuing difficulties in the present. This aim was accepted, and the client felt able to say that she was exhausted and wished to end the session early.

The client came to the second session in a considerably more lively state, and without prompting said she wished to show the therapist some hostile letters she had received from her parents. She voluntarily talked about some very painful family experiences, again finishing the session early but with the comment, 'This has been a good session.' During the greater part of the session she had kept eye-contact with the therapist.

It is clear that both the psychiatrist and the client found their interview unsatisfactory. There seems to have been very little rapport between them; but we would argue that the framework which this professional brought to the situation was strongly normative, reflecting a hierarchic role-relationship in which judgement and decisions were seen to be the corollary of professional expertise, and in which the client was expected: to act in accordance with her patient status; to answer as asked, and to wait for decisions to be made by others about what she needed. Conversely, in her sessions with the NLP therapist, the client had experienced a sense of rapport, had been assured that she was in charge of the therapy's aims and content, and that she could even determine the length of the sessions according to her emotional stamina. The underlying assumptions were very different, and facilitated a very different state in the client.

For us, this example was a telling reminder of the power of what we presuppose. In our view, the assumption in therapy is too often that the client is unwell/dysfunctional/exhibits pathological feelings or behaviour; that this needs labelling and attending to by experts because the client can't even fully recognise what their problem is, still less find ways to manage or improve their situation; that their feelings or behaviours are somehow aberrant as responses to their current or historical situation; that the problem is a static or permanent feature (the client 'has' a condition). And so on. We believe this approach can on occasion actually *limit* the therapist's effectiveness and the client's ability to access their own resources.

Some key beliefs within NLP about presuppositions and their role in therapy

- What we presuppose defines what is conceivable and what is possible.
- It is not possible to function without presuppositions.
- Presuppositions are intimately related to beliefs, and often underpin them.
- Presuppositions help us make sense of the world, and derive from experience as well as formal or deliberate learning.
- They provide us with a working blueprint, rather than exact knowledge, but are often acted upon as if they were factual.
- Presuppositions are communicated indirectly as well as directly (and are often more influential when operating at an indirect level).
- They can be communicated verbally and non-verbally.
- They reflect attitudes and assumptions which underpin thera-peutic work.
- Some are broadly framed, concerning such issues as how the world is and how human beings are (e.g. whether people are inherently self-motivated or lazy, altruistic or self-interested), and relate to what is considered possible.
- Others are more specific, and relate to what is considered 'appropriate', 'normal', 'correct' in relation to specific issues such as patient/therapist roles, the framing of particular therapies or the management of the therapeutic encounter and its context. These may underly procedures and terminologies characteristic of particular therapies (e.g. concepts such as 'resistance', 'ego', 'Parent/Adult/Child').
- Because perception is selective, we tend to filter information according to what is already presupposed, thereby tending to reinforce the original presupposition with further 'evidence'.
- The presuppositions which underly NLP are not considered to be *true*, but rather *useful*. This acknowledges the hypothetical status of all presuppositions, while recognising both their inevitability and their influence.

Milton Erickson, Fritz Perls and Virginia Satir each had significant presuppositions, which coloured their approaches to their clients, their view of their own role and that of the client in creating healing change, and of the very relationship of 'problems' and 'solutions' to the human condition.

Characteristically, NLP first identified or extrapolated and then formulated these presuppositions. In this chapter, we want to explore some of those which NLP has found to be enabling, and which we believe will help give you its flavour. We cannot state too clearly that we believe this kind of presupposition, whether explicitly or implicitly expressed, underlies the work of many good therapists *of whatever persuasion*: by definition, *enabling presuppositions enable*. In the pages that follow we will look at the implications for therapist and client of some of these presuppositions.

Some central presuppositions within NLP

- The map is not the territory.
- People are doing the best they can given the choices available to them.
- Every behaviour has a positive intention.
- The meaning of every communication is the response it elicits.
- There is no such thing as failure, only feedback.

The map is not the territory

A map is a practical resource which helps us find our way around. In its geographical sense, it is a schematic representation of the features of the landscape. It reduces the size and complexity of that landscape and uses a variety of conventions to highlight features considered to be important to the user. Even the same piece of landscape may be represented in a number of different ways depending upon the function of the map: larger or smaller scale, walker's maps, geological maps and so on.

In much the same way, human functioning can be 'mapped out' in many different schematic ways. There are management maps and educational maps, physiological maps and psychological maps, each depicting features which are considered significant within the framework of a particular group of 'map-makers' and 'users'. Psychotherapy offers, among others, Freudian, Gestalt, Jungian, Reichian, and Transactional Analysis maps. The features which are considered central to one may be represented differently on another, or even discounted. Models of the mind are as much maps in relation to the mind's 'reality' as cartographic representations are in relation to landscape. They are working guides, not realities. And as with cartographic maps, their value depends upon their *usefulness*.

NLP does not claim to offer a better map, but rather to say something about mapping itself. One of its consistent messages is that usefulness is the criterion by which all maps must be judged – and that the user can benefit from whatever is useful, whatever map it is found on.

The history of the evolution of the London Underground map illustrates the principle particularly clearly. Early maps of the underground attempted to represent the geographic 'reality' of the system. Because the train lines snaked all over London, the map became less and less user friendly as the system itself became more and more complex.

What was needed was a representation that would be useful to the traveller. From this viewpoint, the map needed to be clear, with the interrelationships between the different lines shown simply. The traveller did not need to know how the lines wandered about in precise relation to the surface above, they only needed to be able to make decisions about where to change and where to get off in relation to their desired destination. A radical new way of thinking was required to create the kind of underground map which we are familiar with today. It was in 1931 that Harry Beck went beyond trying to realistically map the underground railway system. What we now know as the London Underground Map, strictly speaking, is not a map at all: it is a diagram, and hence even more schematic than a map. Beck's inspiration was to offer travellers a diagram of how the system's different lines interconnected. His idea was based on an electric circuit diagram with different colours for each line. Precise distances, twists and turns in the line were irrelevant.

The criterion for evaluating this map is one of being able to understand it so you can use it to get to your destination. Because the new schema turned out to be so useful, its principles have been copied for other transport systems worldwide.

NLP presupposes that any maps relating to human behaviour (internal or external) have an equally schematic relationship to the 'reality' of experience, or, perhaps even more provocatively, that the reality is substantially defined by the way you map it. From this experiential standpoint, nothing is automatically ruled out, or automatically ruled in. NLP concerns itself with *what works*, which may sometimes bear as remote a resemblance to 'above-ground' experience as the Underground's representation of the closeness or distance between stations. The map works for the user underground, but can sometimes distort the different kind of reality experienced by a walker in the streets above.

If the map works in the context, it can be said to be a good map. If a map of the mind helps us do good clinical work, it is at that point in time, for that client, and that therapist, a 'good' map. The question is 'Does it work?' not, 'Is it true?'

Map users get familiar with the maps they use. Probably most of us have experienced some irritation when a favourite form of map (motorists' guides, for example) has been redesigned. We liked it the way it was. Therapeutic map users tend to be the same. The more we use any one map, the greater the tendency that we will assume it is real rather than a mere schematic representation. Once we have done that, we have begun to believe that the map is indeed the territory, and our constructs have objective reality. A transactional analyst whom we knew once said to a group of students he was teaching: 'Just remember, the Parent/Adult/Child model is really useful – but don't be fooled into thinking that everything is reducible to three little circles!'

People are doing the best they can given the choices available to them

When people come for help, they often want to change feelings or behaviour that seem 'stupid', 'silly', self-defeating or self-destructive. Thus, in addition to the aberrant behaviour itself, they often pass judgement on it, or, worse, on themselves. However, as an academic colleague of ours said, apropos his sociological research, 'There's no behaviour, however strange, that doesn't make sense at some level to that person.' Similarly, in a different field, the actor Michael Caine responded to the comment that the villains he played seemed some-how rather likeable by saying that, 'to themselves, no-one is evil'.

Both these observers of the human condition help us turn upside-down any tendency to assume that the client is somehow failing or broken. What happens if, instead, we start to assume that their behaviour and feelings are meaningful, relate to their current or past situation appropriately, even if obscurely, and that in responding that way they have found the best way they could at the time?

An early client of Ian's came seeking help to change his self-destructive behaviour. 'Whenever things are going well for me,' he said, 'I manage to wreck them.' He had driven away his girlfriend, and was currently provoking his work-partner, with whom he had so far had a good relationship, to the point where this partnership, too, seemed likely to fail. He said he needed to know why this was happening. Exploring his history to search out what possible advan-tage this behaviour might bring, Ian learnt that when he was quite little his mother had found she could not manage him and his brother, and they had been placed in a Barnardo's home. They had settled well, and made good friends, finding there a new 'family'. Some years later, on a whim, as the client then saw it, the mother had decided to 'play happy families' and taken the children out of care again. Describing this, he said – without thinking – that from this double disruption he had learnt that 'all good things come to an end'. Here is a belief born of a number of key experiences. It was not one he consciously held. Once articulated it was out in the open but no less powerful. Specific NLP belief change techniques (in particular re-imprinting) were needed to ensure that reasons turned into results so that insight gave way to a change in behaviour.

NLP does not claim that the presupposition that people are doing the best they can is necessarily true, but rather that we get further *if we assume that it might be*. If we take the view that it is ridiculous to reject good relationships, that normal people don't do this, the judgement that this client is in these respects 'not normal' closes down much further enquiry, and prejudicially affects our view of him and his capacity to function in the world. If we assume that his behaviour is meaningful and purposeful, we start to search for what meaning and purpose it might conceivably have. We look, in other words, for the *relationship* between behaviour/feelings and the client's circumstances.

This mindset is exploratory rather than categoric, collaborative rather than judgemental. It helps client and therapist to work together in searching out such possible meanings. Further, it relates closely to the view that behaviour is learnt – and learning can be modified. This approach allows us to respect the client, and the validity of their methods of managing in the world as they experience(d) it, while working with them to open up a wider range of alternatives.

Every behaviour has a positive intent
Like all presuppositions, this is an assumption, not a demonstrable 'truth'. But to assume a health-seeking purpose in the client's actions leads us on to seek out what that might be. If the assumption is that there is purpose, and that that purpose is ultimately benign, therapist and client are free to explore alternative, value-neutral or positive means of achieving the same purpose. If, on the other hand, the assumption is that the client's behaviour is 'self-destructive', 'pathological', 'disturbed', 'silly' or 'stupid', a whole clutter of negative consequences follow. The client feels even more worthless, inadequate, stupid or irrational; therapist and client are further separated by the assumed wholeness/adequacy of the one and the apparent brokenness/inadequacy of the other; and the drive of the therapy is often directed backwards towards the history of the 'problem' (now reified into a quasi-object) and its traumatic origins.

In contrast, the assumption of positive intent leads the work forward, because the frame is *outcome-oriented*. It can be profoundly liberating to a client when their self-deprecating judgement, 'I know it's silly of me, but . . .' is met with a version of 'Hold on . . . what does that behaviour or feeling achieve for you?' This kind of question is often an intervention in itself, since it can disrupt a long-held view of the self, allowing much more enabling possibilities to creep in. What if consistent overeating, for example, might be a learnt pattern of self-administered comfort? Or a way to avert a husband's jealousy through keeping the wife too fat to attract other men? Or a way to buffer a young adult, abused in childhood, against further predatory attention? Or a life-long reproach to the adult world for its treatment of an obese child – look what you did to me?

Recognition of possible intent is not in itself the answer, but the startling notion is often for the client the beginning of a chain of changes. What was stuck has begun to shift. In NLP terminology, it is a 'reframe', attaching a very different meaning to the same set of information. Frequently, the intent of a behaviour is obscure to both client or therapist. Its very obscurity has added to the client's feeling of being out of control, 'I know it's ridiculous of me to . . . but I can't help it'; 'I know I shouldn't/don't need to, but I still do'. There is a profound sense of being at odds with oneself; of an internal alienation from this powerful 'part' which against judgement, logic, common sense and against the person's own wishes appears to be running the show. It may, of course, be the very strength of this internal alienation which is often picked up by others as 'illness', 'pathology' or – in our earlier term – 'brokenness'. The client feels broken, therefore acts as if they are broken, is therefore judged to be broken.

One client came to therapy in a distraught state, fearing that through his 'stupid' and 'irresponsible' actions he was bringing about the end of a long-term relationship. He and his girlfriend had lived together for several years, and he was very clear that he loved her. However, she had recently begun to pressure him to settle down and have children, and he had found this prospect alarming. He was a skilled systems analyst, making a good salary, and also greatly enjoyed being 'one of the lads' – a role which involved playing in a band and periodically getting 'trashed' at the pub. He and his girlfriend had many heated arguments, and he decided to move out for a few weeks to 'sort himself out'. During this time, work took him abroad, and one night he struck up a conversation with an air-stewardess staying in the same hotel – a conversation which progressed to bed and to the anticipation of future meetings. On return, he sought the help of an NLP therapist who had been recommended to him by a friend, and explained what had been happening.

C: I know it's unfair to both of them, and I never meant it to happen, but I just couldn't stop myself. It's like the other night: I went out with the lads and we got absolutely loaded. I don't even remember what happened, but one of them punched the other (he gets aggressive when he's drunk) and put him in hospital. I was so drunk I thought it was funny at the time – but now I feel I don't ever want that to happen again [*gestures with his right hand*]. Yet I can't be sure it won't. It's like there are two parts of me.

T: A part that wants to be responsible, and settle down and have kids, as you've said, and this other part that wants . . .

C: [*Gestures with his left hand*] . . . to have a good time, to fool about like a kid.

T: So there's these two parts – the one who just wants to fool around, get drunk, chat up attractive women . . . [*gestures to client's left*] and the one who enjoys staying at home with your girlfriend . . . [*gestures to client's right*]

C: Yes. I keep trying to suppress the irresponsible one.

T: What's it like when the kid is in charge? [*gestures left*]

C: Well, it's fun. I feel I'm catching up on times I never had. [*The client had said in the previous session that his mother had had MS from when he was quite young, and that he had looked after her before and after school since his father worked some distance away.*] I don't have to answer to anyone. It's not doing any harm. I'm just enjoying myself.

T: But the morning after . . . [*gestures to client's right*]

C: I woke up and felt ashamed – and quite rightly.

T: So you can easily see what the responsible one is doing for you. What about the kid?

C: Well, looking at it now, I suppose he's trying to make up for lost time. I didn't really have a childhood – and he's scared that if I settle down to marriage and kids I never will. So he tries to make sure it won't happen – yet, anyway.

T: So he's looking after you in a different way.

C: Yes, I suppose so . . . Yes, he is, isn't he.

An assumption of positive intent allows for the strong possibility that the intent may be chanelled through behaviours which are dysfunctional, historically outmoded or based on limited or skewed information; allows the client to reconnect with that 'part' of himself which is organising the feelings or behaviour; and allows him to separate out any adverse judgements as relating to the means chosen rather than to the self that chose. This last element is extraordinarily valuable because it allows the problem to be relocated at a lower logical level. It is no longer a question of spoilt identity, a level whose importance and apparent totality makes it often seem fixed and not amenable to change. By contrast, a belief may be modified, a limited capability enhanced or retrained, a behaviour modified or a new one developed. In the session described above, the therapist paced the two conflicting 'parts' by mirroring the client's own hand-gestures – an initial pacing which then became a way of 'cueing' the client to access the intent of each. By this means, the client began to recognise that the part he – and his girlfriend – had considered 'irresponsible' had its own positive intent. This laid the foundation for work which helped to achieve workable solutions while continuing to honour his diverging needs.

In this connection, it can be seen how the psychiatrist referred to earlier was effectively blocking off therapeutic progress by dismissing the client's objectives and reasons as 'vague and generalised'. From an NLP standpoint, her internal monitoring system accurately informed her that things were not right; she was, in fact, able to relate this appropriately to her life experience; but at the time of her interview she did not appreciate that there might be a positive intent to the problem state (depression, lack of affect). Like many clients, she wanted to feel better, to 'deal with the past', and recognised that therapy was a way to help her do this. It was a major surprise to her to be invited to consider that her feelings related appropriately to what she had experienced, and that her behaviour might be considered purposeful.

In inviting the client to consider their 'problem' in this holistic and positive way, NLP also involves them in a shift of perspective which in itself can be freeing and enabling. From an unpleasant immersion in their *first-person* experience, the client is helped – perhaps in a matter of seconds – to shift to the neutral, curious, *meta-position* of being an observer of themselves. Such a shift, reversed, occurs naturally, if sometimes unpleasantly, in self-consciousness: it is a shift, in other words, which we all know how to make. An invitation to become curious about oneself transforms one into a personal anthropologist: how strange this pattern of behaviour; how curious but in its own way logical the relationship between the ritualised or repeated pattern and the intent. Once studying oneself in this non-judgemental way, one can also begin to make comparisons – how do others go about this intent in their patterns? How, in other circumstances, other times, other moods, do or might I? At this point, where the client is engaging actively with their problem, perhaps for the first time, NLP can offer them many tools to help them make the behavioural or feeling changes which they want, while at the same time respecting the underlying positive intent of the original problem behaviour.

Such an approach obviates the need for 'resistance' – a phenomenon which itself acquires a very different meaning. Why would anyone with a positive intent need to resist attempts to change? Answer: because the proposed change might be overlooking, or dismissing, or failing to incorporate, the positive intent. Stop smoking? Great. But what of the positive intent (Be cool or glamorous? Take a few minutes off whenever you need to at work? Enjoy the camaraderie of fellow smokers). Identify and respect the intent, and the client is in a position to seek out other, less harmful, ways to achieve it.

Seen from this perspective, resistance itself is positive and purposeful in intent. The skilled therapist honours resistance by pacing the part of the psyche responsible for it.

Yet surely there must be some issues which, with the best will in the world, can't be seen as having positive intent? How about suicidal feelings? How could the wish to die in any way have a positive intent? Within many therapeutic contexts, the assumption is that suicide is to be avoided, argued against. What happens if, in contrast, the therapist asks the client what such feelings do for them? Maybe they 'make me realise there is something I could do in this impossible situation'. Maybe they 'remind me that I could stop being a burden to others if things got too much worse'. Maybe 'If all else fails I know I can be at peace'. Positive – yes.

Pursuing the question often brings further information – to the client as well as to the therapist.

'And if you did realise there was something you could do . . .?' 'Then I could go on a little longer.'

'And if you remember you could stop being a burden to others . . .?' 'I'm more willing to believe them when they say they want to care for me'.

'And if you know that if all else fails you can be at peace?' 'Then I don't feel so desperate right now.'

Thus an intimate connection is revealed between the thoughts of self-destruction and a positive intent at more than one level:

- Suicidal thoughts → a knowledge of power → going on a little longer.
- Suicidal thoughts → reminder I can stop being a burden → belief in their care.
- Suicidal thoughts → peace is achievable → feeling less desperate.

One important result of this process is that in helping the client to unpack the sequence of positive intents (and there may be even more iterations), the therapist enables the client to respect themselves more and to recognise that their experience and their behaviour adds up.

As with many other processes that work, seeking positive intent, the 'laddering' of questions and the recognition and use of the metaphor of parts are not unique to NLP. What is unique is the coherent integration of these elements into learnable techniques. The claim is not that behaviour really does have a positive intent, only that working *as if it were true* in clinical practice has vitally enabling results, and that techniques or no, this is a way of thinking and can be learnt by both therapist and client.

The meaning of every communication is the response it elicits
Most of us assume in everyday life that we know what we mean, and
that unfortunately other people sometimes 'don't get it':

> Jeremy: I just asked him what he'd said at that meeting and immediately he flew
> off the handle and said I was accusing him of misleading the public.
> Jim: He was really aggressive and accused me of deliberately not telling the
> public about the service he offers.

What is 'the truth' of this exchange? One colleague wants the other to
apologise for his accusations; the other doesn't see any need – 'I was
just asking him what had happened'.

This misunderstanding, like many in all spheres of life, clearly
involves the implicit question: who is responsible for the meaning of
a communication? The implicit notion of responsibility, as so often,
clouds the issue. Was the questioner 'responsible' for upsetting his
colleague? Should he have said the same thing differently? Was the
listener 'responsible' for being over-sensitive? Even if it were possible
to adjudicate, a result so obtained would probably be as fruitless as
many a teacher's decision on many a playground fight.

What happens if we assume that the listener's response tells the
speaker what the communication meant? This removes the issue
from one of intent (what I meant and whether you succeeded in
understanding it) to one of results. In the case of this row at work,
the meaning was an insult, because the listener felt insulted. Never
mind whether the speaker meant to insult him, never mind whether
he was over-sensitive. The response is feedback for the speaker about
what has been communicated. If intent and response are the same,
then the mission is accomplished. If not, the response can be used
proactively by the speaker to help him clarify what is needed next in
order to communicate his intended meaning more successfully.

Again, the implications are forward- rather than backward-
looking. Searching for intent and blame takes us into the past. The
row happened. Recognising that the meaning of the communication
was its effect leads speaker and hearer to consider the important
question 'What next?' The speaker may say that he didn't intend to
hurt, recognising that the listener was hurt. The listener may wonder
how he can check with the speaker whether his understanding of the
speaker's services is accurate, or how he would like it explained to the
public in future. The implications and possible actions lead to the
future.

At a wider level, the speaker may begin to consider this incident
from second position i.e. imagining how it might seem from the other
person's stance. Do other people seem to 'misunderstand' him in a
similar way? Does he need to become more attentive to *how* he

communicates, rather than *what* he communicates? Or is this an isolated incident – in which case he may need to take particular care in future when communicating with this particular listener. The focus of the enquiry, from either position, is on developing more effective communication, not on attributing blame or causality.

What implications does this have for therapy? Most importantly, it focuses the practitioner on the client's *responses*. These become the touchstone of the effectiveness of what is offered. This can sometimes be a humbling experience for the therapist; but it ensures that therapists are consistent in their attentiveness to clients, and sensitive to the amount and nature of the pacing which may be needed before any attempt to lead. The client's response will tell us whether we have succeeded in our attempt to communicate with them.

There is no such thing as failure, only feedback
This presupposition relates closely to the previous one. If the therapist, for example, assumes that an intervention has 'failed' because the client did not respond, or responded adversely to it, they may feel inadequate or inadept. The client, conversely, may feel they have let the therapist down because the intervention 'didn't work'. If the response is framed as feedback, the implication is that something else needs to happen: practitioner and/or client look for other approaches, other ways forward.

If the therapist responds in this way to apparent set-backs in the therapy, they offer the client a powerful model which the client may in turn take forward into the wider context of their life outside the therapy room. The feedback frame is like the curiosity frame in that it offers a way of taking the person out of a possibly unpleasant first-position experience, 'I am/this is a failure', into a neutral one, 'Why didn't that work? What would need to be different in order to improve the situation?' This has a number of important consequences:

● It increases flexibility.
● The person's internal state is no longer compromised by experiencing unexpected setbacks as overwhelming obstacles or disasters.
● Negative feedback is much less likely to be taken personally – it is more likely to be experienced at the levels of environment, behaviour, capability or belief rather than at that of identity.

So what about 'real' failures? The driving test, the interview that doesn't result in the job, the marriage that cannot be retrieved. These outcomes are indeed negative, the opposite of what was hoped for. The point we are making is not that failure doesn't exist in people's perceptions. Rather, that if you look at it for the information it contains, you are in a position to learn, and do, more than if you go no further than the label and the feelings that go with it.

Really engaging with this presupposition is anything but blind optimism: it is a strenuous and sometimes taxing business. You may be concerned with what can be learnt from the event; you may need to consider strategies to prevent any reccurrence. These processes, as with so many in NLP, involve *how* questions, not *why* questions. You are not required to function perfectly, only to pay attention to the effects of your actions. Success is an iterative process. Ideally, each intervention is an improving approximation to what is needed. When you get it wrong that just means you know more about how to get it right next time. The frame is one of looking for the learning in an experience, the underlying belief is that human beings are learners, and learning can be modified.

Let's take an example. A woman in her 50s wanted help with a pattern of binge-eating. She had had glandular problems in childhood, and had a very low sense of self-esteem despite success in her profession. Her marriage had failed, and this added to her sense of personal worthlessness, which she resolutely maintained despite evidence that men found her attractive, despite her size, and wanted to go out with her. The first major therapeutic intervention produced a clear improvement: she stopped bingeing (though she still ate more than she felt she needed), and her self-esteem began to improve. After five or six weeks, however, she told her therapist that she felt she was beginning to 'slip', as she had found herself eating substantially more of her 'permitted' foods than she thought she really needed. She was afraid that the change was not going to be sustained. Although client and therapist both felt that this session went well, the client returned a fortnight later and reported that she had binged again three days previously. She was very downcast. The therapist took this apparent 'failure' as feedback, and explored with the client what benefits there could possibly be for her in stabilising her weight so as to maintain a cushion of surplus fat. 'I can't think of any,' said the client, '– except perhaps to prevent me from taking the risk of becoming intimate with my current boyfriend.' In discussion, it became clear that although the client was very attracted to this man, and understood that he was to her, she felt she had been a failure in her intimate relationships and that it would therefore be safer to remain on friendly, but not intimate, terms with him, even though this entailed her remaining fat and forgoing the possibility of future happiness. This discussion made further work possible, utilising a specific NLP technique that honoured the client's legitimate need for emotional safety and helped her develop ways of protecting her vulnerability, while moving cautiously forward in the relationship and at the same time continuing her programme of weight loss. The apparent 'failure' of the initial intervention had in fact indicated a deeper, and hitherto unrecognised, need which had to be met before the client could achieve what she wanted.

In this section we have explored a small number of key presuppositions which underpin therapeutic work in NLP. Originally derived from the observation of outstanding communicators, these presuppositions and others like them have powerfully enabling implications for therapist and client alike. They help direct us away from the problem toward solutions; away from past events which we cannot control towards the present and future, which are very much within our control. Because they assume and enact an equality among all human beings, they demonstrate and reinforce a personal equality in the relationship between client and therapist. When modelled by the therapist they can also facilitate another very important change for the client because they offer a new way of relating to one's experience and shaping it both consciously and unconsciously.

Conceptual model: problem frame vs. outcome frame

We have shown how crucial presuppositions are in affecting us at every level. They frame our experience. What we presuppose influences what we include in our perception, acting as a filter for available sensory information so that we unconsciously see, hear and feel what we expect. This template of expectations also shapes the way we decide what information is 'relevant'. There is a famous story by G.K. Chesterton, in which a man is murdered in a building – but no-one entered or left. It is only when Father Brown, in his characteristic, apparently naive way, asks simple and obvious questions, that people remember that one person did in fact go into the building – a postman. They had not even considered the postman – they had simply not registered him – because they did not associate postmen with violent crime. It is because Father Brown does not filter through these kind of assumptions that he habitually notices more than other people, and connects information in ways that solve problems.

The way we, and our clients, frame the work we do, has important effects on what happens. We are going to highlight just two kinds of framing here, though there are others.

The problem frame
Clients usually come with a problem frame, as we discussed in the chapter on Change. They have a problem – situation, feeling, thought-

pattern, behaviour, relationship, past. They want to do something about it. It could be the most natural thing in the world for a practitioner to begin work by saying: 'Tell me about your problem . . .', or, 'What's your problem?', or, 'How can I help you deal with your problem?'

At one level, these approaches all pace the client, since they work from within the presenting frame of reference. However, they leave the frame intact. They also leave untouched many other assumptions that go with the frame. Further discussion is likely to occur around:

● the history of the problem;
● the cause of the problem;
● reasons for the problem;
● failed attempts at solving the problem.

The focus of the problem frame is on the difficulty, on explanations, on the past, on how it limits the client and their life, and on feelings of failure and stuckness. (And, of course, as we recapitulate these we reinforce the client's *problem state* at many levels.)

However, it is important to recognise that the problem frame is not a 'bad' frame in itself. It paces the client, and it can also lead to greater clarity about the nature of the problem, its history and its effects. While this information does not in itself bring about therapeutic change, it may nonetheless be useful.

The outcome frame
A characteristic outcome frame question in NLP would be:

'What do you want?' (said slowly, curiously, invitingly).

Long before she knew much about NLP, Wendy used to say to new clients:

'Tell me, what's on your shopping list for our work together?'

Further questions, developing work in this frame, might include:

'How will you get what you want?'
'How will you know when you have got it?'

The famous 'miracle question' in solution-focused brief therapy is also within the outcome frame. The therapist says to the client, 'Suppose that one night, while you were asleep, there was a miracle and this problem was solved. How would you know? What would be different?' (de Shazer, 1988: 5). Adapted from Erickson's strategy of pseudo-orientation in time (1954), this invites the client to make a leap to the far side of the problem, and in so doing to access an unconscious awareness of what needs to change, and perhaps how it needs to be changed.

Clear outcome frame questions emphasise an orientation that is future focused. They presuppose opportunities, change, volition and empowerment. Where failure is an inherent ingredient of the problem frame, within the outcome frame, negative results are more easily perceived as feedback, offering information that helps the client select more effective and productive routes towards their desired goal.

Problem frame questions
- What is your problem?
- How did your problem start?
- What ways have you tried to resolve your problem?
- Why do you think you can't . . .?
- How long have you had this problem?

Outcome frame questions
- What do you want?
- How can I help you?
- What would that do for you?
- What is your greatest ambition?
- What would make life better for you?

Skill-builder

- Try these questions out with a colleague (peer or supervisee), in relation to a real personal or professional issue. Notice the responses you get at a behavioural and state level.
- Ask yourself and your colleague how different it felt to be asked different framing questions.

Presuppositions Skill-builders

Therapist
- For the next ten sessions you do, clarify for yourself, at the time or shortly after the session, whether the client was using the problem frame or outcome frame, and which you were using, in your discussion and thinking.
- With the next five clients you work with, deliberately begin by asking the 'What do you want?' question, with an appropriate empathic open-ended enquiring tonality.

Supervisor

- List the six questions you ask most frequently. Look at what each presupposes, and consider if these are useful presuppositions. Are there other questions which would be more useful?
- Ask yourself, what is the most useful piece of work you have done this week, and why is it the most useful piece of work you have done this week?

Presuppositions Transformer

'What's the most . . .?'
Working with a client one day, Ian became aware that although useful work was being done, the client's body language was demonstrating a considerably greater level of agitation than the overt content of the session seemed to warrant. When a natural pause occurred, Ian leant slightly forward, and in a measured and thoughtful way asked: 'What's the *most important thing* you could say to me today?' The client then began to tell him about a number of very serious concerns which he had not mentioned before, but which had been increasingly preying on his mind. The whole tenor of the session had changed, taking the work, and its consequent benefits to the client, onto much more profound levels.

How had this been brought about? There are a number of key elements:

- The word 'most' invites the client to make *comparisons*.
- The phrase 'most important' directs the client to an internal search: while it is content-free, it nonetheless prescribes a specific class of information that is to be identified – that which is most important to the client.
- The question invites the client to take themselves seriously, yet it also builds in a safety factor: it is not asking the client what's the most important thing they are thinking or feeling, but what is the most important thing they 'could say' to the therapist 'today'. There is still an implicit permission to withhold information, or defer revealing it to another time.
- Yet, within a frame which continues to allow the client all the protection she or he feels they need, there is a firm invitation to say something of major importance.

There are many different ways in which we can make use of this basic structure, as practitioners and as supervisors, just by picking different key words. For example:

What's the most	important	thing you could say to me today?
	useful	thing you could take away from here?
	successful	piece of work you've done this week?
	interesting	discovery you've made about yourself this week?
	challenging	opportunity for you at the moment?

It is important to remember that we can use such questioning to elicit 'good' information as well as 'bad'. An elderly therapist who taught Wendy on her initial therapy training course reported what a huge difference it made – to himself as well as his clients – when he started asking clients 'what's the best thing that has happened to you since we last met?'

3

Modelling

We need therapists who know why they were able to effect a
change in a structure or who can explain why they failed.
(Wilhelm Reich, *Character Analysis*, 1972)

Modelling has been at the heart of NLP from its very beginnings. The
early NLP skills and techniques grew out of early studies of three outstanding practitioners, Fritz Perls, Milton Erickson and Virginia Satir, and
of the way of thinking which they demonstrated in their actual behaviour.
This process of modelling has since been applied in many fields. It works
by seeking models of excellence. At its core is a fundamental question
about all models of excellence and their achievements, viz.: 'How do they
do that?'

Modelling is a basic human process: children model the adults around
them, initially at a quite unconscious, unselective, macro level. As
therapists and counsellors, we spend a considerable amount of our time
dealing with the consequences. Later, modelling may become more
conscious, as when a young child says he wants to be 'just like Daddy'.
With conscious awareness comes the possibility of selective, or micro,
modelling, in which specific traits, abilities or skills are modelled.

Modelling is not imitation. The child walking in the same way as the
parent, developing the same speech intonations, is doing more than
merely imitating: in taking on these behaviours they end up by making
them their own. And when we deliberately model others, availing ourselves of the effective patterns which they use in any sphere of life, our
seeking to understand and replicate their excellence goes beyond imitation also. The child's process is unconscious throughout; deliberate
modelling begins with conscious attentiveness; yet in both cases the
modeler 'gets inside' the experience rather than simply 'tacking it on'.
Sometimes the difference between the two may be subtle: as we shall
discuss later, it is often useful for a therapist, for example, to model out
the structure of a client's problem behaviour, but this does not mean
that the therapist then goes out into the world having taken on that
behaviour as their own. But the attempt to understand from the inside
how that behaviour is structured, how it is to perceive and act in the
world from that standpoint, goes beyond the mere copying of its
external manifestations.

Modelling, in NLP terms, rests upon curiosity, respectful attentiveness to every detail of internal as well as external process, and active involvement in 'trying it on for size' or 'being in someone else's shoes'. It follows that the process of modelling is itself non-judgemental: for the practitioner to model out the client's problem behaviour or thought processes is as valuable to the therapy as it is for the client to model the practitioner's curiosity about the behaviour.

This in turn brings us to another important understanding within NLP: that the therapeutic relationship between client and therapist is a working alliance, rather than an hierarchic interaction, involving both partners in an active mutual attentiveness. This becomes the basis of speedy and subtle mutual adjustments at many levels, which build rapport and trust, leading to an enquiring, experimental co-operation in the work of helping the client forward.

This chapter explores the nature of modelling, its many potential therapeutic applications, and its inestimable significance for practitioner and client. Modelling is the cornerstone of NLP: from its historic roots in the modelling of outstanding communicators via the extrapolation and teaching of the effective patterns which they and other good communicators have in common, it provides us with information about the way in which our experience is structured, and thereby with the means not only of restructuring limiting patterns but also of acquiring and generating new and enabling ones.

The nature of modelling

Modelling answers the question 'How do you do that?' It is both an approach and a method, and can be directed at anything. When, many years ago, Wendy's husband Leo went away on a year-long course and needed to cook for himself, she taught him how to make a basic white sauce, on the grounds that if you know how to combine fat, thickener and liquid, you have the basis for making all sauces. This also illustrates how modelling can be generative: learn the essential structure of any process, and you can apply it, or adaptations of it, in any situation to which it has relevance.

It also demonstrates how a major outcome of modelling is *teaching*. Making a recipe, keeping accounts, a turn in skating, successfully managing a meeting, conducting an interview, learning foreign languages, making someone welcome, looking on the bright side, being able to forgive, sustaining intimate relationships, sleeping easy at night, experiencing grief and then gratitude for having had a loved one in your life; all have a structure (or perhaps many possible structures). These structures can be observed, broken down into processes and sequences, and taught to others so that they too can do it. Equally, anxiety, panic attacks, jealousy and depression have structures, some features widespread, some more individually tailor-made. Modelling these structures and sequences allows what has been experienced as indivisible, unavoidable, overwhelming, to be taken apart. Once the structure is known, all kinds of possible changes, modifications and updates become possible. If a pessimist says the bottle is half-empty and an optimist says it is half-full, by finding out how they each get to that point we can discover structures which help each to have more choices.

Modelling also allows us to begin to intervene at the level at which the problem is being experienced, rather than necessarily having to 'dig deep' for its origins. A client who reported that he often felt that his face was becoming 'frozen' and 'wooden' was asked to notice what happened when he remembered a compliment someone had paid him. Immediately he smiled. Asked to first access the frozen feeling, then immediately think of a compliment, he found an immediate change in his internal landscape, as well as demonstrating rapid external changes in expression, skin tone and colour. Taking this process into life outside the session, he found that he was able to replicate the change in feeling and expression for the better whenever he noticed the frozen feeling. A fortnight later, he said that the process was becoming more automatic, so that he was having the frozen feeling much less and finding that he was smiling, more mobile in expression and more cheerful much more of the time. He was also noticing that work-colleagues did in fact pay him compliments more often than he had supposed, and was beginning to be convinced that, as these were quite unsolicited, they must be genuine.

This raises the interesting question: just how superficial is super-ficial? In this client's case, there was indeed a long history of depression and poor self-worth, explored in, but not much alleviated by, long-term and intensive psychotherapy. He felt he had become stuck, which was his reason for seeking a different approach, but nonetheless he still believed that his lack of self-worth was so severe that much time would be taken to improve it. Yet what seemed a very simple, surface procedure, not only made significant differences to how he felt, but gave him an experience of a change being really quite easy. This offered new choice at the level of beliefs: it destabil-ised his belief that any change would be difficult and protracted. It also began a cascade effect, so that he began to filter external infor-mation differently as well.

That was not the end of the therapy, but it was the beginning of a turn-around from a vicious circle to a virtuous one. One part of the structuring of his depression had included the sequence of: being in a place where others were present → frozen face → negative self-judgement → anticipating that others, seeing the frozen face, would also judge him negatively → feeling cut off and distant → becoming more withdrawn. Into this sequence we had inserted one new item: frozen face now → remembering unsolicited compliment, which in turn → smiles → face becomes mobile → feels better about self → recognises that others will see him smiling and may think him friendly or approachable → and so on. Because human identity is systemic, change in one part of the system can bring about changes throughout the system as a whole, as this client was beginning to find. Finding that he could get a change quite quickly changed his expectations about what could happen and just how soon he was going to let it.

This example also demonstrates how one can model self: 'How do I do poor self-worth?' opens up the possibility of 'how I might do greater self-worth?' Modelling also allows us to avail ourselves of the expertise of others, and to enrich our own experience through taking on the way they do theirs. It is important, of course, to recognise that this process has realistic limits: age, physique and life experience will condition the extent to which we can replicate a skill demonstrated by someone significantly different. Sometimes the test is not whether we can do whatever it is they do, exactly as well, but whether our modelling of them produces a transfer of knowledge such that we now have an enhanced ability. A client was asking for help in preparing for an interview. Her family had been very isolated and withdrawn, and she felt ill-at-ease in social situations, anticipating that because of this she would be tense and make a poor impression. Asked if she knew anyone who had the kind of outgoing ease she wanted to demonstrate, she immediately identified a relative and a work-colleague. From modelling how they would behave at interview, she was able to improve her own performance.

It can even be possible to model at a less specific level. Another shy young woman found herself having to be responsible for collecting contributions for a colleague's leaving-present, choosing, ordering the gift and finally presenting it. She was very struck by the irony that she, the least outgoing person in the group, was having to perform these tasks, but said to herself: 'How would an outgoing person do it?' What she was modelling was her own internalised understanding of outgoingness. This in turn alerts us to a highly significant principle: whatever is felt as real, is real in our experience. This young woman had a choice of 'realities' available to her: that of her personal previous experience (shy, diffident, quiet) or that of her stored knowledge of outgoingness observed in others. Faced with a situation which called for confidence and social ease, she chose to enact that internal reality rather than continue with her historically experienced one. In this sense, it can be seen that modelling is about choosing another available reality.

As a process, modelling is neutral. Human beings are brilliant natural modelers, modelling the limiting, self-destructive and disabling as easily and effectively as the enabling and life-enhancing. This too can be an important realisation for clients, since it helps them locate their 'problem' at the level of structure which seems more amenable to change rather than at the level of identity, which is felt to be integral, 'given' – and also precious, 'a poor thing, but mine own'. However, the more relativistic our notions of 'reality' become – the clearer we are that reality is for each of us what we make of our experience, rather than the experience itself – the easier it becomes to appreciate that modelling is a tool of genuine transformation. Whether we deliberately seek to model specific skills and behaviours (conscious micro-modelling) or unconsciously take on a broad range of characteristics from some influential context or other (unconscious macro-modelling), modelling is at the heart of growth, learning, development and change.

As we have shown, we can model whole or part, self or other. We can also model directly or indirectly. The sports person who approaches a situation as their trainer would is modelling directly. Someone asking themselves, 'How would Granny have done this?', or, 'How would Plato have seen this?' is modelling indirectly their understanding of the approach of those individuals.

Here, the modelling might be very specific or perhaps very generalised. Plato's – or Granny's – values may be what the person is seeking out in their immediate situation: tuning in to those values will guide their actions. The internal repertoire of models upon which we can potentially draw is immense. The test of the modelling is the difference it makes in practice. Knowing how Plato would view a moral dilemma is not the same as being guided by his values in making your own moral judgements. The one is an intellectual process: find the Plato file and see what it says. The other is an internalised, taken-on-for-real process: react as we imagine our Plato would react were he here.

We already know this on an everyday level of course. Those of us who have lost important family members may well find ourselves referring to them in our own internal conversations years after their deaths: 'I know just what Dad would have thought about this'. Important professional or academic achievements may be enhanced by our knowledge that our old teacher or first boss would take delight in them. Pop icons, or characters from literature, all people this internal world of significant others, and are potentially available to us as models. An elderly lady wishing to give up smoking described how she had first smoked as a teenager much influenced by movie icons, lamenting, 'It seemed so elegant then, you see, dear.'

In a professional sphere, Ian, in his Master Practitioner training refers to this account by Rachel Naomi Remen of profound and extensive modelling in the daily work of Carl Rogers:

> Years ago, I was invited to a seminar given by Carl Rogers. I had never read his work, but I knew that the seminar, attended by a group of therapists, was about 'unconditional positive regard'. At the time, I was highly sceptical about this idea, but I attended the seminar anyway. I left it transformed.
>
> Rogers's theories arose out of his practice, and his practice was intuitive and natural to him. In the seminar, he tried to analyse what he was doing for us as he did it. He wanted to give a demonstration of unconditional positive regard in a therapeutic session. One of the therapists volunteered to serve as the subject. As Rogers turned to the volunteer and was about to start the session, he suddenly pulled himself up, turned back to us, and said, 'I realise there's something I do before I start a session. I let myself know that I am enough. Not perfect. Perfect wouldn't be enough. But that I am human, and that is enough. There is nothing this man can say or do or feel that I can't feel in myself. I can be with him. I am enough.'
>
> I was stunned by this. It felt as if some old wound in me, some fear of not being good enough, had come to an end. I knew, inside myself that what he had said was absolutely true. I am not perfect, but I am enough. (Remen, 1989: 93)

This illustrates modelling at several levels: Rogers is self-modelling, in that he is benchmarking the session he is about to begin by reference to his internalised belief-in-practice. Remen's experience and her account of it model Rogers. In offering this, usually first by reading it aloud, Ian models it to practitioners in their next level of training. The validity of the experience is clearly demonstrated by Remen's statement that the experience has 'transformed' her, and in turn by the response of many of Ian's students, who report a sense of greater connectedness with their practice clients in the training, and a greater sense, when in client role, of feeling at ease and being attended to. And, of course, each therapist, from Rogers himself along the chain, models this belief-in-action to the client. For if it is enough for the therapist to be human in the presence of the client, it follows that, *mutatus mutandis*, it is enough for the client to be human in the presence of the therapist.

It is of great interest to us in another way, because Rogers tells us precisely how he structures his internal experience. He doesn't *see* himself working well, *feel* good about it and then begin to work; he doesn't *feel* moved by the individual's situation and then *imagine* being able to help non-intrusively. What he actually does is to *let himself know* that he is enough, and then he can *be with* the client. He first engages in Internal Dialogue (lets himself know), and then can 'be with' the client, which indicates a shift to Kinesthetic (body or feeling) processing. NLP has developed a form of notation which enables us to describe such sequences economically and exactly: once we have this detailed access to internal processes, and its specific sequencing, we have a means of transferring knowledge and replicating behaviour. The result is what are known as strategies. In other words, we have at our disposal the very structures of excellence.

Modelling in NLP therapy

Modelling is characteristic of NLP because it is an active process. Perhaps one might also turn this around, and say that NLP is an active therapy because it is based on modelling. In this, as in other ways, there is a parallel between client and therapist: both learn by doing. This is aptly reflected in the designation of the initial major training in NLP as the *practitioner* training. The basic question 'How do you do that?' attunes the student to the development of attentiveness and observation, to processes, structures and their relationship to outcomes. Training provides experiences which integrate the acquisition of knowledge and its enactment. Similarly, therapy alerts the client to the question of 'How do you do that?', develops attentiveness to processes and structures in the experiences of self and others, and to the relationship these have with outcomes. Work in the practitioner's office and in the 'real' world outside provides contexts in which learnings of all kinds are integrated into internal and external action.

Let us recap the key processes at work here:

- respectful attentiveness;
- a learning frame;
- the identifying of patterns and sequences, and breaking them down into their constituent parts;
- modelling effective patterns.

Attentiveness provides the base on which the interaction takes place, a base of rapport in which the therapist can first pace, then lead, the client. Conversely, it is the attentiveness of the client to the structure of their own experience which makes possible a shift from their initial helplessness in the face of their problem to a state of almost anthropological enquiry, and provides the evidence that it is 'what', 'where', 'when' and 'how', which, far more than 'why', identify the constituents of the problem and thus open up the possibilities of exactly keyed-in change factors. Pharmacological research is currently utilising the body's natural matching of transmitters and receivers as a model to develop precisely targeted interventions. In a similar way, once the shape of a problem behaviour is known at the level of its constituent parts, it becomes possible to target any one of many key parts with a precisely matched intervention. The modelling of the problem provides the structure of the solution. In fact, as we will show later in more detail, it is our clinical experience that the problem behaviour encodes the solution quite precisely.

So far, we have been talking as if solutions need to be individually tailored. While every client is indeed unique, NLP has, however, identified a number of strategies with a broad range of application – because many problems, whatever their specific details, share common structures. People develop phobias in relation to many different stimuli, but the structure of one phobia is essentially very similar to that of another. People have many different reasons for not being able to spell easily; but all good spellers have certain strategies in common. For these reasons, NLP procedures, like the fast phobia cure or the spelling strategy – which may at first glance tax credulity by their rapidity and apparent simplicity – can be guaranteed to work at profound, rather than superficial levels because they are built upon precise modelling of the problem, on the one hand, and a successful strategy on the other. This modelling, together with the interventions necessary to help the client make the desired changes, has provided us with elegant, economical and repeatable therapeutic procedures.

Effects of a modelling approach to therapy

- A modelling approach sets up a mindset of curiosity in the therapist: this is usefully humbling, and focuses attention on the client as individual rather than on the client as type.

The importance of modelling is that it enables us to engage in active enquiry and exploration, which is non-judgemental. The presupposition is that there is a structure to problem behaviour, and that this will be individually determined rather than categorically predictable. Once a problem behaviour is seen as a set of learnt skills, the presupposition for the therapist is that the client does indeed have skills, even if they are presently being employed in ways which cause problems. At an implicit level, this affirms the status of the client.

- A modelling approach teaches the client to take a meta-position in relation to their own problem experience, thus helping them to recode what has hitherto felt stuck or locked.

When the client begins, with the practitioner's help, to unpack the structure of an unwelcome experience, they necessarily change their relationship with that experience. It is likely that in the past they have been trying to avoid, suppress or reason it away, that they may have been condemning it, or themselves, for experiencing it. Asked now to pay even more attention to it, but with an enquiring, scientific approach, they will automatically change their vantage point in relation to it. This is a significant intervention in itself.

- Modelling involves the client in active enquiry and experimentation, which provides an empowering and refreshing contrast to 'learnt helplessness'.

Many clients tend to reify their problem behaviour as though it were separate in some way: often they will talk of a 'part' of themselves which drives the behaviour. They might even say things like 'I don't know how to stop my brain doing this . . .', or, 'That voice keeps telling me . . .' The process of observation and enquiry relocates the client's sense of self in a more neutral area in which they can begin to re-experience a sense of activity and self-direction: it is potentially an area of mastery rather than helplessness.

- The emphasis is on the process involved in the problem, which is value-neutral, rather than on the consequences, which have been negatively valued.

Focusing on the 'how' of the problem changes the client's orientation towards it, from one of avoidance of the problem outcomes, to one of active engagement with its processes. At an emotional level, this helps the client shift from negative feelings to more neutral and progressively more positive ones. It also allows them to recognise that the processes in which they are engaged are not negative, even if the outcomes currently are. This too allows them to reclaim as 'normal' significant amounts of their own functioning.

- Pathology is reframed as a set of specific skills learnt by the client.

Where many clients will have learnt to think of themselves and their behaviour as damaged, abnormal, illogical – to have assumed or accepted what Erving Goffman in his book *Stigma* (1963) called 'spoilt identity' – they will be enabled through a modelling approach to recategorise their difficulties as those of behaviour or belief, rather than those of core identity. This is an intervention in itself.

- Once the structure of a problem experience is known, it can be deconstructed.

Two important points follow from this. Firstly, the client has often been unaware that the experience did actually have a structure. Familiarity with the automatic nature of the experience is likely to have made it seem both inaccessible and almost unchangeable: it 'just happens'. To recognise that it has a precise structure and sequence, and to be the prime collaborator in seeking that out and describing it, is an immensely empowering experience for the client. Secondly, identifying the separate building blocks of the experience offers the possibility of deconstructing and then reconstructing the whole.

- The basic assumption is that the behaviour makes (made) sense and is therefore at some level both understandable and acceptable.

For most clients, to understand that behaviour is a learnt response which relates in specific and appropriate ways to life experience is to feel rehabilitated in their own eyes. Behaviour ceases to feel inexplicable and out-of-control, even if it remains undesirable or outdated. Learning to reclassify problems in this way involves the client in a deeper analysis of their own functioning and how it relates to past and present circumstances.

- Once recategorised in this way, problem behaviour/feelings/parts no longer need to be split off or condemned: thus a reintegration becomes possible.

Through this approach, the practitioner models an acceptance of the client *as a whole*, a process which, like many before us, we have identified as being central to the client's own self-acceptance, and thus to their recovery.

- A modelling approach suggests the possibility of transfer of skills from other areas of the client's experience, as well as from external models.

One important feature of a modelling focus is that therapist and client seek out not only the structure of what doesn't work, but also the structure of what does. Through the process known in NLP as 'contrastive analysis' they are likely to explore related situations in which the problem doesn't occur, or where the client feels very different, and to uncover their structure. Once the structure of positive, successful, life-affirming experiences is known, the client's own success-structures can be replicated and transferred into other contexts. Once learnt, this process of exploring for effectiveness can be carried out by the client independently, thus generating further development and self-empowerment.

- Change becomes effortless and rapid, relating effective patterns to the individuality of the client.

The shared understanding of the structure of the client's problem experience which is built up between practitioner and client allows them to develop a collaborative awareness of the points of maximum leverage. Therapeutic interventions, being thus precisely targeted, are more likely to be economical, brief and lastingly effective.

- The client is empowered.

Many of the processes first engaged in collaboratively in the counsellor's office can be taught to the client – or will have become part of their learnt repertoire through the very power and efficacy of those collaborative experiences. The client thus goes away with more choices, more skills and more possibilities than they came in with – and more than relate to their original problem issue.

- From an understanding of the relationship between the uniqueness of each client and the patterns which underlie classes of problems and their solutions, the therapist develops greater flexibility and creativity in their own work.

It is important to realise that a modelling approach to therapy is enabling for the practitioner as well as for the client. Training and experience will have equipped the therapist with conceptual, theoretical and experiential frameworks which guide their understanding, help them assess information and select appropriate interventions. However, the high degree of individual focus which the modelling approach involves helps ensure that, from a range of possibilities, the client dictates, through their language and reactions, what the most appropriate intervention will be, and how its effectiveness will be demonstrable. At one extreme, we could say that this ensures that the therapist has the pleasure of reinventing the therapy for each client in every session. Less dramatically, we might claim that this invites flexible, creative and appropriate exercise of the practitioner's own unique experience and skills.

Let's look at an example of how modelling can be used in therapy to help the client, and how rapidly within a single session the client can begin to access the differences in their own internal strategies and external behaviours that make a difference. A client was seeking help in preparing for his examinations to qualify as a solicitor. This particular examination seemed to involve a great deal of rote-learning, since he had to memorise the precise legal wording of a number of documents in order to be able to quote them exactly.

He found this extremely boring: his concentration kept wandering and he had made little progress. He felt he should be able to motivate himself better.

T: Can you tell me what it's like being unmotivated – what happens exactly? You know you ought to do some study . . . what then?

C: Whenever I think about it during the day, I tell myself [Internal Dialogue] that I must really work hard tonight. And I try to imagine myself doing it . . . but all I see is those endless paragraphs of black text, and that great fat file waiting to swallow me up.

T: So you're *telling* yourself you *should*, and you're *seeing* all that black print. How is it when you're seeing it – large? small?

C: I don't know . . . well, now I think about it, it's small – squiggly and rather too fine to see easily – there's too much detail for me to focus properly on it.

T: So it's already difficult when you imagine it in your mind's eye?

C: Yes, that's right.

T: And when you get home, what happens then?

C: I make a cup of tea – look at the paper, tell myself I deserve a bit of time off, all that kind of stuff – anything rather than get down to it. Sometimes I doze a bit in front of the telly. Then I get cross with myself for wasting time. So then I'm in a bad frame of mind – irritated – when I do sit down to look at it. My eyes just look at the stuff, but it doesn't go in. I can sit there and sit there and suddenly realise I haven't got the faintest idea of what I've been supposed to be taking in.

T: So you do all kinds of things to put it off, and then you're just staring at it without it going in. Your eyes are working, but there's no connection?

C: That's about it.

T: Can you tell me about a time when you were really motivated to learn something?

C: Yes. I wasn't a swimmer at all until I was in my teens – we didn't do it at school and my family weren't into it. When I was about fifteen and hanging about with a good crowd I realised one summer I was missing out. We did everything else together, but it was hot and they were off swimming a lot, and I thought I'd really like to do it. So I promised myself I'd do it secretly – learn and then just turn up one day and join in, like I'd never not been able to. I found an intensive course – every day for a fortnight, just to start beginners off. Early evenings, after school. Kept imagining how it would be when I could do it like the rest of them. Didn't tell anyone. After that I practised some more, joined an ordinary class. Couple of months later, nice day, someone suggested going – and I just went along too. Surprised them all just like I'd planned. I really felt good about that.

T: So you *felt* you were missing out, and *promised yourself* you'd do it secretly. Then you put in a lot of work, just *imagining ahead* how it would be when you'd learnt it. You'd made *yourself a promise*, and then *got that vision ahead of you* to work towards.

C: Yes, that's how it was.

T: So when you do do something you want, first you tell yourself, or promise yourself, something about it, and then you see in your mind's eye how it will be when you've achieved it.

C: Yes, I suppose that's how it is.

T: So that's a strategy that works for you?

C: Yes – and now I come to think of it I used it once for something I didn't really want to do.

T: Tell me about that.

C: Yes. When I was coming up to A levels I realised I'd need Chemistry to qualify for the university course I wanted. And I'd hated that at O level – but there was no way round it. So I thought, what if I pretend I like it and want to do it? And I told myself I'd be really glad when I got that A level and could get that university place – my parents would be really pleased. And I kept seeing myself looking at the result on the school noticeboard – a decent grade – and then the letter from the university confirming my place.

T: So there's an extra element to your sequence, then: the reaction of others. First your friends about the swimming, then your parents about the A Level. Yes?

C: Yes.

T: And how are you doing that bit? Are you seeing them, or what?

C: Yes – their faces – but also hearing them saying I've done well.

T: Great, now we've got a strategy that works – and even better it's one that you already know works. And we know something about how that's different from the strategy that doesn't work. With that one, you're telling yourself you *ought* to do something, and then *seeing it as difficult, or not clear*. And with this one, the one that works, you *feel* you want to achieve it, you're *telling yourself* from the beginning *how good it will be*, you're *seeing* yourself achieving and people you care about being pleased. So: what has to happen now for you to *feel* you want to pass this exam, *tell yourself* how good that will be, and see that happening and others reacting positively . . .?

Self-modelling

We have referred a number of times in this section to 'self-modelling', and it is worth unpacking this concept in more detail to reveal its value to both client and therapist. At the outset, the concept of modelling seems to invite us to look for models of excellence outside ourselves: the implication is that we can learn/improve our own performance by understanding how others, who are better at the skill in question, go about it. Indeed, this outward focus has much to offer. But an equally valuable process is to be clear about what *we* ourselves do well – and this applies equally to counsellor and client.

As therapists, we may have a pretty good sense that we are good – even excellent – at what we do: our clients seem to feel we are in rapport with them, they get better, they comment positively on our work together. This leads to good feelings, but it is nonetheless rather vague. If we apply a modelling approach to our self-evaluation, we can learn more about the structure of our own excellence. Exactly at what point did the client's expression change? What exactly had happened just before then? How had we phrased our last comment – or was it perhaps something we did rather than said? If clients tell us that they feel at ease with us, how exactly do we go about achieving that? What is the sequence of the way we welcome them? Or did the sense of being welcome perhaps begin with a first telephone conversation – or even with our answerphone message? Perhaps we are particularly good with older people, or teenagers? How do we do that?

It is very easy to be aware, through discussion with colleagues, experiences at seminars, reading professional literature, etc. of what we don't do; and this can be dispiriting. This is another reason why it is helpful to establish what it is that we do well – and what it is that we as unique individuals do well.

Self-scrutiny is one way of collecting information that will help us establish the structure of our excellence; but we can also ask others. Sometimes it is appropriate to ask the client. One of Wendy's teenage clients, asked what she found most helpful about their sessions together, took time to reflect then replied the next week: 'This is the only place where I can say whatever I like and be listened to.' Reflecting on this feedback made Wendy very aware of how much teenagers, in particular, value being able to describe their experience and reflect on it in an accepting adult context, and helped her realise that this, perhaps more than many specific interventions, was what was helping her young clients. This in turn meant that she was particularly careful to pace this group in future, deliberately offering them plenty of silences, more thinking time and more non-verbal affirmation.

Asking friends and colleagues what they think you do well can also provide useful information. Again, it helps to pursue the question beyond the first – often general – reply. 'You're not afraid to confront', or, 'You really come across as concerned', can be even more informative if the speaker is able to tell us how specifically we do our confronting in a helpful way, or how precisely we communicate our concern.

When we get into the habit of self-modelling our own excellence, at whatever level of training or experience we are, we are more secure and feel more resourceful when we do need to recognise our limitations. Knowing what you do well means that you feel more comfortable – and more resourceful – about acknowledging mistakes, addressing areas in which skill needs developing, or in taking the 'risk' of additional training. Both of us have found as trainers that students become more confident in trying out new skills and procedures if they do so in a context which has already encouraged them to become alert to their existing proficiencies. Implicit, in such a context, is the belief: 'I can do that'.

This is also an invaluable message for the client. Where the client has realised that their problem has a structure, can be seen in fact as a highly developed set of skills – even if frustrating, limiting or outdated – they are likely to generalise this at an unconscious level to a deep understanding that they have many skills, some of which will be neutral or positive in their results. This allows the client, both at a conscious level and also unconsciously, to engage in an important sorting process. Not just, which of my skills have 'good' results, but, 'How does the application of a skill lead to a good result?' For example, the therapeutic axiom that 'obsessive clients will respond to obsessive interventions' indicates a level at which this process is recognised in the therapeutic community. How much more enabling, though, if we redescribe obsessiveness as the capacity to formulate and repeat detailed and exact sequences of thought and action. Lawyers, historians and surgeons all need a bit of this. So does a pilot flying hundreds of people across the Atlantic. The problem is not in the sequences of action, nor in such a thing as a 'personality-type', but in the application of them, and, even more, in the feelings of distress and being out of control which may follow from that application.

A modelling approach allows the client to recognise, perhaps for the first time, that their unwanted behaviour is a particular kind of skill; that there are likely to be situations – perhaps many of them – in which it can be useful, invaluable or even essential, and to begin to wonder about how the particular problem application is structured presently, and might be structured differently in future to lead to different consequences. The client, as we have said earlier, finds themself taking an external or meta-position stance in relation to the problem as they engage in this enquiry, which is in strong and enabling contrast to the first-person problem frame they are likely to have come in with. The implicit basis of such a frame is that the problem is agreed to exist and the therapeutic task is to remove, heal or otherwise alleviate it. The modelling frame, on the other hand, is one of enquiry and – in Erickson's word – 'utilisation'. The therapy is on a very different footing.

Making this point in an indirect and powerful way, Ian once asked a client to watch the movie *The Dream Team*, which concerns a group of mental hospital inmates taken on an outing by their therapist. Quite accidentally, the therapist witnesses a crime while they stop for petrol, is wounded and fails to return to the van. One of the inmates eventually realises what has happened, deduces that the therapist (by this time in hospital) is in further danger from the criminals, and leads the group to rescue him. It becomes evident that their individual pathologies, combined with the intimate knowledge of institutional processes which they had acquired as inmates of the mental hospital, are precisely what makes it possible for them to work the system and rescue their therapist from the hospital where he is about to be murdered. After watching the movie, Ian's client commented thoughtfully: 'It's funny: everything they did that meant they got locked up ended up helping them save their therapist's life.'

The therapist as modeller

Finally, it cannot be stated too strongly that the practitioner has a crucial role in therapeutic modelling to the client. Here, we are talking about being a model (as in role model), or modelling a behaviour, that is to say, demonstrating it. Erickson, Perls, Satir, Rogers and many others have pointed out that one of the client's major difficulties is that they often despise, devalue, split off and condemn aspects of themselves. Those aspects may be problem behaviours or feelings, irrational thoughts, or even their former actions and identity. Rogers, for instance, argued that one of the most significant things the therapist can do for the client through their interaction with them is to show respect for and acceptance of these 'unacceptables' (Rogers, 1967, p. 63). To model unconditional positive regard is to demonstrate a different way of being. While one may recognise the merit of such an approach the question may arise – 'How do you do that?' It may be a question for the trainee therapist or counsellor, or for the client who wishes to engage with themselves differently. In both instances, having an understanding of the structure of unconditional positive regard would be enormously useful because it would make it possible to teach this as a skill. This is where modelling, in the sense of unpacking the model of excellence, could really be of assistance. In this instance, Rogers has already offered us some of the key pieces in the quotation given earlier.

As a role model, the therapist or counsellor can also choose to model behaviours which may seem negative: for example, a therapist might model a teenage client's anger with their parents by telling the parents that it is time for them to 'get out' of the therapy room. This helps establish rapport with the client, in enacting 'unacceptable' parts of the teenager's psyche, such as hostility and confrontation. At another level, it offers both teenager and parents the possibility of recognising that these feelings, and their expression, may have a valid, and survivable, expression.

Because they are modelled there and then, here and now, in the interaction between them, the 'how to' of many interactional skills are clearly, transparently demonstrated, and can be learnt both consciously and unconsciously by the client. This is another of the aspects of excellence which was identified and explored – overlapping as it does into rapport, pacing, leading and utilisation – at the outset of NLP: it is present in all enabling therapies. An outstanding practitioner commented to us that this is one reason why so many different therapeutic approaches all 'work': the key factor, he said, is not the therapy but the therapist. However, as with so many characteristics of excellence which NLP identified and made part of its explicit framework and teaching, the modelling of how to establish and maintain rapport can be observed, its structure identified and taught to others. And the 'others' include, first and foremost, the client.

Conceptual model: contrastive analysis

As we have shown, the concept of Modelling involves a number of significant presuppositions:

- experience, both internal and external, has a structure;
- we can understand the structure if we have the tools to explicate it;
- when the structure is known, it can be replicated;
- the structure can also be taught to others – the knowledge can be transferred;
- we can use this in order both to learn effective structures from others and to intervene in limiting structures so as to destabilise and then reconstruct them.

One invaluable tool for ascertaining the structure of an experience is to compare it in great detail with another experience which is similar but has significantly different effects. NLP calls this process 'contrastive analysis'. Many people, for example, find it relatively easy to be assertive over issues which involve others – friends, family or employees – but much harder, or even impossible, to be assertive when the issue concerns themselves. Someone in this position can be asked to think of a situation where they were assertive on someone else's behalf, and another which involved themselves, and to describe in detail the interconnected sequence of external behaviours, internal sensory processes, and emotional responses of each. Careful contrastive analysis would allow them to identify where the significant differences lay. Sometimes, in this kind of case, it is in beliefs about relative worthiness – an external person 'deserves' fair treatment but I don't. Or perhaps it is to do with what the person says to themself, their 'internal dialogue': 'I remind myself that it is my job to look after my employees/my child and their welfare', contrasting with, 'Why make an issue of this, it will only make you unpopular'.

When we engage in contrastive analysis, the process requires that we pay extremely close and detailed attention to the available information across a range of dimensions. This is needed for the process, but it is a learning experience in itself which has benefits in many other contexts. Further, it requires that we are attentive to broad issues (large chunk) and to points of detail (small chunk). Because of the personal uniqueness of our structuring, the significant differences which make all the difference to the result are no more likely to involve large than small chunk information: they may involve both. Large chunk is not 'more important' by virtue of being large. Issues of belief or identity are not inherently more significant to outcomes than details of behaviour or environment. All information, in this kind of painstaking search, is potentially equal: what is important is to identify what is *effectively* the determining difference or differences.

Modelling Skill-builders

Therapist
Adopt a 'teach me' frame:

- Model something a client wants to change. Become curious about how they do it, assuming it to be a skill. Imagine you wanted to learn this skill: what are the essential tips needed to operate this kind of negatively valued behaviour/thinking?

NB: Just what would you need to know how to do inside if you were to be able to replicate this unwanted behaviour? In order to explicate the processes involved, the client has to examine the structure of their own problem process from an outside position, which results in a new relationship with the problem.

Supervisor
- Deliberately encourage some of your supervisees to self-model. What are they really good at? (Supervisees invariably bring problems to supervision: this approach reframes and widens the purpose and outcome of supervision.)

Modelling Transformer

The difference that makes a difference
Take one example of something which is not going as well as you would wish, and another related example of something which has gone well in the past or is going well now.

4

NLP and Mind–Body Work

> Some day it will probably be proved that every organ inferiority
> may respond to psychological influences and speak the organ
> language, that is, a language expressing the attitude of the indi-
> vidual toward the problems confronting him . . . Sometimes one
> organ, sometimes another, is outstandingly responsive to the
> pressure of outside influences. In this connection it must always be
> remembered that the organic structure is a unity, and that a shock
> in one area throws the whole body into vibration.
> (Alfred Adler, *The Individual Psychology of Alfred Adler*, 1964: 308)

The Anglo-Saxon poets called the body the 'ban-hus' (bone-house) – a
metaphor which reflects the view, prevalent over the centuries, that the
body was some kind of a container inhabited by the mind, spirit or soul.
Like all metaphors, this one is not neutral: it encapsulates a whole mass
of possible implications.

Another, rather later, metaphor, reflects the development of a
rationalistic, mechanical age: people began to enquire what 'makes us
tick'. If God is the clockmaker of the universe, Man's body can be seen as
a wondrous piece of machinery also. Just as clocks work from the inside
outwards (what appears on the face is governed by the mainspring
within), so the implication for the 'workings' of the person remains much
the same: the inside governs, is responsible for what appears on the
outside.

Recent scientific research offers us new metaphors as it discovers
more and more about the exquisitely complex interrelated systems that
we are. The 'ethereal' mind can be investigated, its hidden secrets
stimulated by electrodes or changed by chemicals, its familiar and idio-
syncratic thought processes unmasked as a series of impulses along
habituated neural pathways. It no longer seems to reside in the head,
even: neuropeptides act as messengers that inform and control transforming processes at many levels, with cascading effects throughout the
system. The discovery of DNA has shown us that every cell carries the
blueprint for the rest. The thighbone may be connected to the hipbone;
but we are a mass of interconnections, most of them far more subtle
than this. And the connections themselves interconnect.

The systemic approach to personal organisation, and to dysfunctions
in that organisation, is one which underlies NLP, and which makes it

especially fluent in working, not only with issues which cross the old mind–body divide, such as psychosomatic symptoms and illnesses, but also with more clearly physical issues. The respectful, attentive curiosity which from its beginnings has been the hallmark of NLP, provides therapist and client with a subtle, precise range of information that underpins their joint work for healing and change. Rapid, complete 'cures' from life-threatening illnesses are not the daily stuff of work in NLP any more than they are in any other therapy (nor are they foreign to it, either); but the working assumption of a personal, systemic inter-relationship of all systems provides therapists and clients with great possibilities for improving well-being and health at all levels and for marking, testing and evaluating the efficacy of their work.

In this section we shall look at five main aspects of mind–body work in NLP:

- the assumptions that underlie the work;
- the features of clinical intervention;
- some specific examples of mind–body issues and strategies;
- the role of belief in determining outcomes;
- the implications for the therapist's own self-maintenance and development.

Underlying assumptions

Ernest Rossi, in his seminal book *The Psychobiology of Mind–Body Healing*, published in 1986, brought together discoveries in neurobiology and years of clinical understanding of altered state work (including hypnosis) to consider the relationship between mind–body states, learning and healing. Clinicians on both 'sides' of the old mind–body divide owe a great deal to this pioneering formulation of what actually happens to bring about state-dependent learning and change. From Deepak Chopra's inspirational *Quantum Healing* (1990), through to articles for health professionals considering the psychological correlates of IBS, eczema, asthma and even cancer, scientific and psychological understandings are increasingly based on the working assumption that we get a lot further if we consider the person as a whole, systemic organisation. Today, even some mainstream medical books pay attention to the mental and psychological components of physical illness.

NLP had its roots in enquiry and description rather than in philosophy or religion, and the systemic view is one which yields important therapeutic benefits. It offers us as clinicians an ideal approach to working with mind–body issues, basing our interventions on informed attentiveness to minute and minute-by-minute variations in the client's subjective experience and externally observable behaviours.

If we assume that the individual organisation is one of interconnected systems, then it becomes obvious that what occurs in one part of the organisation will have effects elsewhere. Whether the organisation is ineffective, dysfunctional, damaged or damaging, or simply 'stuck', the choice of intervention is dictated by what is *accessible* and *what works*. Change brings about other changes. There is an immense economy and elegance in this. Further, as we have said elsewhere, the notion of what is 'profound' or 'trivial' is rendered largely meaningless. If a long-lasting pattern is effectively changed in a single session *it is no longer part of the person's internal structuring*. The assumption that a long-lasting problem has to be addressed by a correspondingly lengthy treatment falls down completely.

For example, Jim, a client of Ian's, asked for help in re-presenting himself for an assessment for a very senior post. Intelligent and able though he knew himself to be, and a good match to the post's requirement for someone capable of both creative and critical thinking, he had found himself floundering in the assessment, his answers rambling without apparent point or structure. Both he and his assessors were disappointed: they wanted him to succeed as much as he did. Previously a fit and active man, he was also upset that he had stopped exercising – he was unfit, flabby and overweight. Ian suggested that if Jim's current work schedule only permitted very brief personal time, he might consider keeping a skipping rope in his car, and either skipping for one or two minutes or running for five minutes whenever an occasion presented itself: he would feel better, he could find this amount of time easily, and he could begin to build his fitness again. Ian also asked him to focus on these feelings of helplessness and inadequacy. When had he felt like this before? Jim responded that he was sure he had felt like this, but felt there was some kind of block on remembering the occasion. Ian then told him how unconscious processing can continue even after a session is over and that sometimes he felt a session really began as the person left.

When Jim returned the next week he had two things to report: firstly, that although he became breathless after running for five minutes he felt both more agile and more alert, and 'like I am getting back in control'. Secondly, he had woken in the night before this session and remembered a very significant event from when he was about 12 years old, which he had never told anyone, not even his parents or his wife of over 20 years. He had been remorselessly bullied at school, and had tried to stay away. Eventually the school had insisted that he return, and his parents had agreed on a day when he must go back in. That night he became so desperate that he took as many aspirin as he could, hoping that he would never wake up. However, he had not taken anything like enough, and woke in the morning with a severe stomach upset and a raging headache. In this state he went in to school, with a traumatic secret to add to his other painful experiences.

Identifying the episode allowed Jim and Ian to begin other healing work; but the foundation for lasting change (which resulted in Jim's promotion to the board) had been laid in that one first session.

Another corollary of the systemic view is that instead of trying to determine what the emotional component of a physical condition might be, what trauma might lie behind its origins, or what it is 'trying to tell us', we are free to work with the condition *in its entirety*. We can elicit information from the client about how they experience the condition at every level, and we can add to this a range of information derived from acute, moment-by-moment, sensory observation. The assumption here is that what the client tells us comes from their conscious awareness and processing: what their posture, expressions, muscle-tone, colour and gesture tell us is equally informative – but comes from another level of processing. Dave Dobson, an old hypnotherapist, called it, with more neutrality if less economy, the 'other-than-conscious-mind'. Neither is inherently the source of 'better' or 'worse' information; yet if both are taken into account, the totality of the available information is richer and thus more reliable. In particular, habitual sequences, characteristic states, and the relationship between changes at any level and the immediate context of the situation, give an invaluable commentary upon the meaning the individual is making from what they are experiencing. Small unconscious physiological changes and spontaneous connections and comments are particularly useful in offering us a running commentary on the effectiveness of our work.

One of our clients had been coming for regular, but well-spaced out, sessions for a number of months, seeking help in managing stress at work. She was an independent consultant and trainer, who also worked regularly with one particular agency. While some of the staff of this agency appreciated her work, others resented her independent status and influence, and this led to problems with information, decision-making and co-operation. She had discussed these issues with her therapist, and evolved effective strategies to manage them and to prevent herself being overly drawn into overt conflicts. However, we noticed that from time to time she would be suddenly struck down by a cold or a virus, or simply by exhaustion. She was inclined to attribute this to exhaustion from overwork, recognising that from time to time this would compromise her immune system and make her vulnerable to ambient infections.

On one occasion she phoned to apologise for being unable to come to therapy: earlier in the week she had been to an important meeting in London, the purpose of which had been to negotiate a major project which she was planning and co-ordinating. The following day she had woken aching and feeling nauseous, and because of this had had to cancel the next two days' work. Though she had hoped to attend our session, she found in the morning that she was little better and needed to remain in bed. In fact, it was from bed that she phoned.

T: It sounds like you really do need to stay in bed and look after yourself. But before you ring off, tell me quickly how the meeting went on Monday – I know it was an important one.

C: It was. I'd heard through the grapevine a few days beforehand that they were very positive – I even got an idea of how much they might be offering to fund the project – so I went feeling I was really well prepared. When I got there they'd changed the deal on me – I still don't know exactly why, though no doubt it relates to the usual problems we have. I found that what they were prepared to offer was only half of what I'd been led to expect, and now they're wanting to add in all sorts of other conditions over and above the proposal we've been talking about. I was really angry and disappointed.

T: That must have been a real letdown . . .

C: Yes, it was. Actually, I'm inclined to think that was what let the bugs in: I thought I was doing well to have avoided the flu so far this winter, but maybe this made a chink in my defences.

T: So having gone there feeling good about things . . .

C: . . . I came home aching with disappointment and feeling sick about it all . . . My body's telling me just what a pain it is! . . . And that's what I often do, don't I? . . . I'm going to think about this some more. Maybe I'll work on this when I come next. OK?

T: Of course. Get better soon.

While this was overtly only a conversation about cancelling an appointment, it was possible to make use of even this brief exchange to help the client forward. Talking with the therapist anchored her into a state of curiosity about her own mind–body experience and its relationship to 'outside' events, allowing her to reach an important understanding about how she often expressed the stresses of her work. The existing rapport with her therapist meant that minimal pacing and leading encouraged her to make the connections, laying the foundation for the next step in the work together. In ending the conversation, the therapist's good wishes could also be taken at an unconscious level as an 'embedded command' with a multi-layered meaning.

This rich information is available not only to the therapist: clients can be taught to pay attention to it too. For the client, this is frequently an exciting as well as empowering process.

Once clients have learnt to pay attention to this important class of phenomena, they can learn the principles of working with them. Usually, the process of learning begins in the deconstructing of a problem experience, perhaps in conjunction with examining how a different, benign experience is constructed. In this contrastive analysis, clients can learn what are for them the significant sensory systems, and what, within these, are the significant sub-modalities.

A client who was terrified of a certain firm's distinctive container lorries came to realise that the terror was directly associated with their colour, and that this enlarged and brightened them in her eyes. She commented that she hated orange, never wore it and had nothing in her house that was that colour. In scanning internally to identify where such a strong association might have been learnt (the process NLP calls a 'transderivational search'), she immediately recognised that the colour was the same as that of her parents' kitchen – a place of hostility and childhood misery. Once the link was identified, work could be done to heal the childhood trauma – but the colour of the containers faded instantly in her mind's eye, and their power to terrify vanished there and then. The client had learnt a valuable technique for exploring the origins of current experience which could become a lifelong resource. The understanding of how this specific experience was encoded, however, yielded far more, since she learnt the importance for her of visual processing (and within that the particular aspects of size, closeness and brightness), and was able to use the knowledge creatively to enhance other experiences. Not only was the knowledge of wider use than the context in which it had been learnt, but it could be used generatively as well as curatively.

An outline of the transderivational search procedure is given as the Skill-builder at the end of this chapter, and ways of working with the detail of how we structure our ways of representing the world to ourselves internally constitute the Transformer.

Features of clinical intervention

Since NLP always presupposes that any work is systemic, working with body–mind issues is not a class apart from other kinds of therapy. However, it may be convenient here to note some features which are distinctive.

- Body–mind work can be done anywhere.

Ian recently helped his wife with a painful knee (a recurrence of an old injury) while on a flight to the States. He asked her to be attentive to the pain, and observed that as she did so, she consistently looked in a particular direction. She said that as she paid attention in this way, the knee got warmer, and the warmth began to spread to the rest of the leg. When Ian then asked her to look in a different direction, she became aware that the feelings became less pronounced. As he encouraged her to continue with this process of exploration, she became aware that when she looked in the first direction again she had a sense of space – 'Life could be easier'. As she considered this possibility, her knee became less tight and painful. They continued to explore these existential issues, and the knee became more comfortable: though she had previously found walking quite painful during the next few days she was able to walk for considerable distances exploring a city that was new to them. The work of healing they had begun on the plane could be continued in other contexts: at a physical level with the assistance of a physiotherapist, and internally at the level of personal meaning.

- Work in NLP can be done in parallel with other body work.

As this example shows, it is easy for an NLP therapist to help a client with some aspects of physiological conditions while an individual is also receiving help from allied health professionals. We have frequently worked alongside allopathic physicians, acupuncturists, homoeopaths, herbalists, and physiotherapists, either independently because the client has sought two simultaneous kinds of help, or through mutual referral. Work of this kind may address conditions which are clearly 'physical' as well as ones which might be seen as 'psychosomatic'. A client was referred by her doctor for help in healing a deep and painful anal fissure. The therapist elicited from the client that she 'saw' the fissure as a deep and angry cleft, and asked her how it needed to be. The client could see the healthy flesh as being pink and smooth, and could imagine the heat and stabbing pain that she felt becoming cooler and less intense. Concentrating intently upon this desired state several times a day brought about a healing process which the patient's doctor judged remarkably rapid.

- Significant improvements can be made in serious or even life-threatening conditions.

Most clients with major illnesses or injuries will already be receiving allopathic treatment. However, in NLP as in other therapies, there have been documented cases of improvement where conventional approaches have failed. Robert Dilts, in *Beliefs: Pathways to Health and Wellbeing*, describes how he worked with his mother, who had had a recurrence of breast cancer which had metastasised to virtually every bone in her body, and whose doctors had said they could do no more than make her comfortable.

> My mother and I spent four long days working with her beliefs about herself and her illness. I used every NLP technique that seemed appropriate. It was exhausting work for her . . . As a result of the work we did with her beliefs, she was able to make dramatic improvements in her health and elected not to receive chemotherapy, radiation treatment or any other traditional therapy. At the time of the writing of this book (7 years later) she is in excellent health, and there have been no further cancer symptoms. (Dilts et al., 1990)

In fact, she lived for a further seven years – a total of 14 from having been given a few months to live by her physicians.

• NLP will work on mind–body issues at the level of meaning which is relevant for the client.

As with any problem, the therapeutic approach will utilise and work with the client's personal structuring of their experience. We each have important constructs about health and illness and about how they relate to issues at the different logical levels. For some, as for Dilts' mother, the key level is one of belief: beliefs can either maintain a view of the inevitability of an illness' progression, or a view of the organism's ability to heal and grow. A recent client of ours had suffered five strokes in rapid succession, which had left him paralysed, and his doctors told him he would never recover. However, he was both determined and rebellious, and was not inclined to accept what he was told by any authority figure. Within days he was struggling from his bed and around the hospital ward; he then discharged himself from hospital and, having no faith in the doctors there, sought the help of a private physiotherapist, who helped him to structure a programme of recovery. Asked where this stubborn determination had come from, he said that he had been told as a youngster that his asthma was life-threatening. Later in his teens, he had disobeyed the War Office notices warning him off a training area where there were unexploded bombs, and had taught himself to defuse the smaller ones: 'after what I'd been told about my asthma, nothing else seemed so dangerous'. Therapeutic work with him on another physiological issue in his late 60s needed to respect and harness this self-preserving awkwardness.

Another example concerns a client referred by her doctor for help with her persistent migraines – a condition often associated with emotional overtones. It emerged in the first session that the client found her domestic situation trying, as a condition of her marriage had been that her husband's mother should live with them. The mother-in-law had never conceded her primary 'rights' in her son to her daughter-in-law, and the menage was often tense and uneasy. The therapist taught her a very effective NLP strategy – the Meta Mirror – for understanding the situation more fully from a variety of perspectives and learning how to take a more distant, less emotional stance in relation to it. The client reported considerable improvement in the relationship with her mother-in-law, and a decreased frequency in the migraines:

C: Things are much better now. I can see her as a poor old thing, frightened to let her son go because she's invested so much in her role as his mother.
T: And what difference is that making for you?
C: Mostly, things are better and I'm more equable with her too.
T: And when she's doing what she used to do – insisting on her rights and her place and on you waiting on her? How are you responding to that now?
C: Not quite so well – I'm trying to put it behind me [gestures to the back of her head] – oh, look at what I'm doing. So that's what the migraines are about. It's when I'm trying to put her behind me. But I can't, not really, can I? I need to find a better way than that!
T: And what would you like that to be?
C: I think I'd really rather just rise above it all, like you showed me with the meta-mirror. I don't need the migraines to tell me what she could make me feel – or what I could make myself feel about her! I know she's a pain – so why not give up feeling it or trying to suppress it and just get on with seeing it differently?

This client made a link between her migraines and her relationship with her mother-in-law, identifying her almost literally as a 'pain in the head'. Once she recognised that she had been perpetuating this experience by trying to 'put it behind me', she felt able to choose a more effective strategy which she had learnt in the therapy. The therapist was able to work within the client's framework and facilitate the process of change and empowerment by questions directed at how she was constructing her experiences, and what she would need to do next. Some years later they met by chance in the street, and the client reported that the migraines had not recurred. Happily for her, her mother-in-law had recently decided to move to a rest home, and the client was very willing to accommodate her husband's frequent trips to visit her in return for a home of her own at last.

● The history of the complaint is not necessarily needed.

Clients with physiological problems have often been the rounds of other professionals, and are likely to have spent a considerable amount of time outlining the history of their complaint and various attempts at treatment. Since NLP assumes a systemic encoding of the difficulty, a therapist can begin wherever an opportunity is offered. It may be at the level of belief, or with a description of how it feels, or with an enquiry about what the client really wants. Not only does this make for much more economical working, but it facilitates 'live' – and therefore potent – work. Each time we describe something, we encode it further in the linguistic and ideological frameworks we are using – and for many clients who have been taking their difficulty around to various professional helpers this will mean that the problem is by now deeply layered and much less accessible. The liveliness, immediacy and often unexpectedness of NLP give client and therapist a way of accessing the issue immediately and freshly, so that effective work can begin immediately.

● Once is enough.

The immediacy of this approach, while giving us access to the encoding of mind–body issues, also bypasses the risk of retraumatising the client through asking them to recapitulate distressing or traumatic experiences. Accidents, injuries and illnesses do not have to be recapitulated in painful detail, but their meaning and legacy can nonetheless be effectively changed.

The role of belief

A number of the examples we have given illustrate how important beliefs are in issues of health and illness, and it may be useful to focus specifically on this dimension here.

At the most fundamental level, belief is what creates meaning out of experience. From our earliest days, we are pattern-making creatures seeking to make sense of our world. The patterns we create are often generalisations which help us to explain and to predict. The process is essential to us – but it is also potentially limiting and distorting, since belief is not in itself fact, but a theory about 'fact'. This is the key both to its limiting potential, and conversely to its power to bring about change. Change the belief, you change the meaning – and thus the 'reality'.

This is probably the reason why most therapeutic approaches work for some people: the approach fits with their belief structure, and they are therefore able to utilise what it offers. We would argue that since NLP is based on eliciting the client's map and working with it, this enlarges the number of people whom it can help. There is no danger of needing to teach the client a particular therapeutic model before we can engage meaningfully.

Let's look at a number of key health-related issues involving belief.

The match to the client

When she was little, Wendy had a wart on her left thumb, which proved resistant to all forms of medical treatment. She received drug therapy to reduce it, and conversely to encourage it to 'grow out'; had radiotherapy; had it cut off with scissors, and treated with diathermy. Regular sessions at the local outpatients occupied Wednesday mornings for many months. Applications of steak which were later buried had no more effect. The wart remained, neither larger nor smaller, until she was in her mid-20s. At this time a boyfriend wrote her the following rhyme:

> Wart upon my Wendy's thumb
> Bugger off to kingdom come.

And it did. With later knowledge, we would say that the irreverence of the rhyme, and its affectionate tone, were sufficient to destabilise whatever belief-structures were holding the wart in place. Clearly, everything else had been tried – and overkill had proved inadequate. Only something radically different could dislodge the wart's status. The therapy has to fit with the client, and it needs in some way to reflect a respect for the client and the problem while not buying into the assumptions of inevitability or permanence. Much health-care work is predicated on the same principles as that underlying the escalating wart treatment: if the problem resists this, we have something stronger. But the often unrecognised implication here is that the strength, resistance, significance of the problem also escalates with every failed treatment. The combat metaphor leads us from hostility to enmity, from cross words to bombardment. The beauty of the rhyme was that it was outside that metaphor entirely.

Clearly, it is too simple to argue that this approach would cure everything; but what we can say is that where beliefs (norms, accepted patterns) are involved, a refusal to work within the holding framework is often a vital step in destabilising it; in opening up the possibility of other ways of perceiving the situation; and thereby of freeing the client to engage with other possibilities at the mind–body level. The task for the clinician is to retain, and express, a genuine respect for the client's presenting framework (otherwise they will lose rapport) while at the same time not buying into it.

Phobias

A phobic reaction is an extremely heightened physiological state in which the sufferer experiences a rapid escalation of helpless terror. Suppose a client is phobic about flying: from an NLP viewpoint what is so encouraging about this, and indeed any phobic response, is that one has only to begin talking about flying and the response is triggered. It is clear then that the client is able to generate this response without the aid of an actual flight. So if we can understand how the client is able to consistently achieve this effect we can then change that structure and end the phobic response.

While a variety of useful explanations have been posited for their existence, we have been struck by how frequently phobias have simple historical origins. In such instances it seems that from an original experience, often a 'one-off', the client learns to protectively generalise their fearful avoidance of similar stimuli, in the process often extending the scope of what is feared. What is fascinating is that to think about the phobic trigger, or to describe it to another, is to set off the reaction. A client who as a very small child had seen his pregnant mother kicked in the stomach by his drunken father, and had forgotten this traumatic experience, came as an adult seeking help for a phobic reaction to balloons. By using a simple trans-derivational search (see the Skills-builder at the end of this chapter) the client was able to locate the source of his phobia. Following his phobic feelings back to their origin brought up the repressed – and to him starkly unexpected – memory, one which was confirmed, even though his mother was by then dead, by another relative. Throughout the 30-odd years after the original event, the client had been terrified of balloons: at the time of seeking help he had a job at a prestigious hotel in which there were many celebratory events involving balloons and though he did not have to be present in the function rooms he found even the idea of the balloons produced such marked phobic responses that he felt he could not endure the situation any longer.

The fast phobia cure in NLP was formulated in response to this characteristic structuring of belief and experience. However, it does not require knowledge of any presumed first event to be effective. Because the response is so rigidly encoded, and so reliably structured, it can be readily destabilised and recoded, so that in an astonishingly brief time a distressing and often increasingly pervasive pattern of response can be eliminated. Change the structure which holds the belief in place, and the experience must be different. In the example above it is literally the case that the client walked in with his balloon phobia and left without it.

Allergies

Allergies are the physiological equivalent of a phobia – a rapid, repeated overreaction to a specific stimulus on the part of the immune system. It is not surprising that a specific NLP technique has been developed for working with allergic responses. Yet here too belief has been identified as a key factor. Belief is all-important, as illustrated by a client of Ian's who began sneezing and wheezing on her arrival in a reception area graced by a huge vase of extravagant flowers. Her amazement when Ian told her that the flowers were in fact artificial rapidly gave way to an intent curiosity at how the 'allergic' process was working, and in turn to work which transformed her responses. A different, but related, process is demonstrated when allergic changes in the blood can be demonstrated to have occurred although the individual shows no overt symptoms. Clearly, there is space for various kinds of intervention here.

Wendy's teenage daughter was allergic to hay, but loved riding. When she was at the stable yard, she would start to sneeze and her eyes would water. One day, Wendy noticed that her daughter was scratching her arm, and that it was covered with little red bumps. She commented that this looked like an allergic response, but that she hadn't been aware of it happening before. Her daughter explained that, knowing from her A Level Biology that the body could show various forms of allergic response, she had decided it would be less inconvenient to have red bumps than to sneeze all the time.

Another friend also loved riding. As a teenager, she too had suffered allergic responses at the stables – but these had been tested and attributed to an allergy to horses themselves. Nonetheless, she continued to ride until she left school, when finance became a problem. For many years she did not ride, but when she later took up the sport again she was surprised to find that she no longer sneezed. Considering why this was, she was surprised that the answer which immediately came to her was, 'I don't sneeze because I'm not frightened of horses any more.'

Allergies are fascinating and can be complex, but as these examples illustrate, more is involved than a 'mere' physical stimulus–response process.

Placebos

The word 'placebo' is often used with a derisory tone, as though somehow it isn't 'real'. Yet the actual point is that – whatever the assumed mechanism – the changes a placebo brings about are *real*. Are we really arguing, then, that unless a change is brought about by mechanisms we can understand and logically account for, it is somehow spurious? This is an untenable position. If what the client is after is change, then change which successfully occurs has to be acceptable.

If a patient is given an inert substance believing it to be pharmacologically potent, and gets better, we have to posit the operation of a systemic mechanism. This has been demonstrated not only in the obvious cases of giving people inert powders to combat conditions needing medication, but in the case of telling people that a drug which, for example, lowered blood-pressure, was one designed to raise it – yet their blood-pressure responded in the direction they believed it would go in, rather than in the one the drug was designed to influence. There is certainly scope here for the kind of change which NLP helps clients to bring about.

There is another way in which we, as therapists, need to be concerned with the placebo effect. People in positions of trust and authority carry huge influence with their clients. A colleague of ours calls this the 'prestige effect', and it casts an interesting light on transference. Where there is a combination of anxiety, vulnerability, dependence and authority, anything which is said or done by the authority figure will carry weight with the client out of all proportion to the surface meaning. It may be useful for us as therapists to assume that we have this potential with our clients all the time: that we in ourselves constitute a placebo for them. The client/patient invests the placebo with meaning, and the effects are proportional to that investment.

An example from one of our supervisees illustrates this. A businessman came for help at a crisis point in his business and personal life: he was facing a boardroom takeover, his marriage was falling apart, and he was becoming involved with a colleague at work. He came for three or four sessions only during the height of the crisis. A couple of years later, he left a message on his therapist's answer phone: 'I've taken your advice: sold the business, broken off the relationship at work, divorced my wife, moved to a different town and bought a flat and a new business. Would you like to come to my housewarming?' The therapist remembered very clearly that no such 'advice' had been given – simply, the sessions had explored what the client really wanted from life. But in reaching his decisions, the client had 'heard' his own judgements as stemming from the therapist, and had framed them as 'advice'.

When clients come to see us, it is important that we remind ourselves that they come with expectations: our reputation, for example, may have attracted them. Though we know this to be based upon 'training and experience, as it reaches out into the wider community it may well have the powerful attraction of a placebo: take this therapist once a week for ten sessions and you will get better. Does this invalidate the skill of our work? Of course not – but it is certainly an ingredient in its effectiveness!

Mind–body and the therapist

We have already argued that therapists are significant models for their clients, both consciously and unconsciously. This applies in the mind–body area just as vitally as in any other, and there is as much need for personal as professional congruence. What messages does the client implicitly receive from a therapist who, for example, is overweight, smokes heavily, looks pale, tired and exhausted and whose concentration is variable and apparently distracted by other concerns? The therapist's baseline working state needs to be one which facilitates their ability to work with the client attentively, with appropriate levels of energy, modelling a healthy, self-nurturing lifestyle.

We would argue from our experience that this involves modelling the same mind–body behaviours that we believe to be enabling to the client. We help them by modelling a rounded and enriched lifestyle which respects ourselves at every level just as much as by offering them our skilled clinical experience. Specifically, we believe that we need to be concerned about enhancing as well as merely maintaining our physical health, taking care that we have leisure and room for a private life, exercising as well as eating in a nurturing way, building our own best relationships, developing interests and activities that have nothing to do with therapy. We need time to reflect or meditate, time to be creative and playful, time for involvement with friends and family, time to be alone.

If these are some of the elements of a rounded and enriching lifestyle, we need them too – because these give us a life worth living and at the same time demonstrate through our active, positive modelling that this kind of a life is achievable. This is one of the most important ways in which we show our clients that life after therapy is more than just the absence of the presenting problem: it can be even better than they dared to hope.

Conceptual model: states

A state is the totality of our way of being at any given moment. It involves:

- neurological activity;
- physical energy;
- general activity;
- emotions;
- mental activity.

In itself, a state is neither good nor bad – but its outcomes can be appropriate or inappropriate, enabling or limiting. We all get accustomed to particular states, and are less consciously aware of these than of ones which feel different or less characteristic. The common phrase 'being in a state' tends to get used to describe an agitated, unpleasant state, yet there are people for whom this could be called a habitual or 'baseline' state, just as there are others for whom it is very uncharacteristic.

There is often an implicit belief that a state 'just is': that it occurs in response to external events or circumstances, or is even part of who we are. The knowledge that we can change, choose or create states can be a very enabling part of therapeutic learning. Let's take some examples:

- A busy working woman pursues her active hobby in the evenings and weekends. Sometimes she is aware of saying to herself 'I can't do this properly tonight – I'm not in the right state of mind.' She learns to identify what, for her, characterises a 'right' state of mind for her hobby, how that differs from one appropriate for her work, and how to make the change she wants from one to the other when she wants.
- A health-care professional who originates from Ireland lives and works in the UK. After a visit home she comments: 'It's really difficult adjusting when I come back – I talk faster there, I'm more fun-loving. I can get from Dublin to my workplace in three hours door-to-door, but it takes much longer than that for me to adjust to who I am.' She learns how to use the available time to adjust the key variables so that she feels more 'in sync' with her environment when she returns.
- A computer software designer comes for help, exhibiting severe tension. He works in a high-pressure, high-profile company demanding long hours. He can't relax, can't sleep. Asked about non-work time, he says he works out at the gym and plays squash. His high-pressure state carries over from work into play. He learns to identify what would characterise a more restful and refreshing off-duty state, and how to build ways of triggering it.

In addition to learning ways of changing from one specific state to another, we can also become curious about states we have not yet experienced, model others who already exhibit them, and explore what their benefits might be in our own lives.

Mind–body Skill-builder

Transderivational search
Definition: 'The process of searching back through one's stored memories and mental representations to find the reference experience from which a current behaviour or response was derived' (Dilts, 1990). Whenever you find that a response is inappropriate to the structure triggering it, you can know that the past is running the present. By taking that response and tracking back on it you can locate its source. As you track the response back, you may be aware of experiences which you 'knew about all along'; but you are also likely to be surprised by remembering some which you had long ago forgotten. This is because the search occurs not only at a conscious level, but also at an other-than-conscious-level, and it is the information which has been held out of consciousness which surprises us as it surfaces again. The response you are tracking is the linking and identifying thread.

Therapist
● Say to your your client quietly and authoritatively: 'Take this feeling and ride this feeling back into the past', or 'Let this feeling take you back to where it *really* belongs'. Use a supportive voice, one that is not intrusive. Space out what you say. Watch your client, and allow them to take the time they need. Wait for their response, without offering additional comment, until it is clear that they have said all they need to say.

Supervisor
Viewed from an analytic perspective, this is an extremely useful tool for eliciting counter-transferential material. Cues to use it with your supervisees might be when they are: irritated, powerless, helpless or over-involved in relation to a particular client.

● Encourage your supervisee to have a clear experience of the (counter-transferential) feelings or thoughts. As they do so, you can say: 'And as you pay attention to these feelings (thoughts), let these feelings (thoughts) take you back in your own life to where they really belong . . . So that you can just pay full attention to them . . . and know all that you need to know about them . . .'

There is no reason why, as a supervisor, you shouldn't also be assisting your supervisee to understand their positive counter-transferential feelings also; for example, where they look forward to seeing a particular client, or feel sad at the prospect of the client terminating therapy with them. The same invitation to ride it back into the past might prove very informative.

Mind–body Transformer

Working with sub-modalities
Every experience is uniquely coded by the brain in terms of its structure and its content using the senses – visual, auditory, kinesthetic, olfactory and gustatory. These five senses are sometimes known as modalities. Within every sensory system there will be finer discriminations. Each picture, sound, feeling, and so on, will have – quite apart from the actual content – its own structure, which consists of various qualities. These finer discriminations are known in NLP as 'sub-modalities'.

We make meaning of an experience not only from the content, but how we represent the content to ourselves in terms of its structure – its sub-modalities. Part of the meaning will depend on the structure. We will probably have some kind of response to the experience – we will feel something *about* it. This means that if we change the structure then the meaning and feeling will change accordingly.

Some key sub-modalities:

- Visual: distance; size; colour; tone; brightness; contrast; focus; movement; associated/dissociated; edge (framed or not).
- Auditory: distance; volume; pitch; tone; tempo; clarity; harmony.
- Kinesthetic: internal/external; pressure; texture; temperature; humidity; size (area); duration; speed; still/moving; rhythm.

Take a mildly unpleasant experience and notice the sub-modalities you use to represent it to yourself. Now begin to change some of these and note which sub-modalities have most impact on changing how you are with this experience. For instance, if you are conscious of your recollection having a visual dimension and it is in colour, change this to black and white; if it is close to you in your mind's eye, move it further away. Experiment and you will find certain sub-modalities will be critical.

Take an enjoyable or 'good' experience, and identify the sub-modalities by which you currently encode it. Vary these one at a time, noticing and retaining those changes which improve your representation of the experience.

5

The Client–Therapist System

> Energy and attention have gone into forcing yourself, because of a mistaken feeling of 'oughtness', along lines that run counter to your healthy interests. To the extent that you regain and redirect this energy, the areas of restored vitality will progressively increase. It is nature that cures – *natura sanat*. A wound heals or a bone knits by itself. There is nothing the physician can do but clean the wound or set the bone. It is the same with your personality.
>
> (Perls, Hefferline and Goodman, *Gestalt Therapy*, 1951: 112)

The title of this chapter highlights a very important assumption in NLP: where it is customary to speak of the 'client–therapist *relationship*', we want to draw attention to our understanding that the interaction between the two constitutes an active *system* created by and between the two individuals. As with other systems, there is mutual influence, and, as the word 'system' implies, there are also implicit and explicit structures which affect both parties. There are assumptions (about the nature of the role each has, about the purpose and process of therapy, about change, about the self) and there are rules. While some are overt (for example, what happens if either party has to cancel, how payment is made), others, although not spelt out, are present nonetheless – Does the therapist interpret? What amount of silence is acceptable? In what ways is it acceptable for the client to influence the therapist? Perhaps the most significant implication of a systemic approach is that interaction between the two parties is recognised as mutually regulating: therapy is not a treatment which the client 'receives', the therapist 'gives' or even 'offers', but rather an ongoing collaborative dance.

In this chapter we will look at some features of the client–therapist system which are characteristic of NLP, and which may differ in emphasis, or perhaps not even exist, in other therapeutic systems.

The client experiences being taken seriously

We want to make it clear that by 'seriously' we do not mean 'dourly' but rather 'respectfully'. We give our clients our best attention – but this can be expressed in a range of ways and tones, at times including humour. A client's difficulties warrant our concern and our skill; but we do not serve them as well as we might if we invariably treat them with a dolefulness equal to their own. Provided the client feels we are in rapport with them, there can be a place for many different emotions in a therapy room if they are congruent with helping intent and personal respectfulness.

Probably all therapists would claim to take their clients seriously in this sense – but do they in effect? Our client, who encountered the psychiatrist we mentioned earlier, said afterwards that he had made her feel she was 'a head case'. Her welfare officer, who had attended two interviews with her, reported that the psychiatrist had 'undone two years of my work with the client' by telling her, firstly, that her mother had 'mental troubles', and secondly, that her sister (who committed suicide) had mental troubles and therefore it was very likely that her own mental troubles were genetic. While no doubt the psychiatrist believed that this opinion was supported by his training and experience, the client was emphatic that she had not been taken seriously, but rather belittled and deprived of any sense of power to change her situation.

But even where therapists do communicate to the client that they are taken seriously, an additional message may also be that they are taken seriously as someone who is limited, malfunctioning or broken. Improvement in their condition is likely, as a consequence, to be assumed to be conditional: they can become less limited, function slightly better, or be mended. How different does it feel to receive at many levels the message that one's way of coping makes sense, that one could learn to cope even more effectively (and without some of the hitherto undesirable side-effects of one's current coping strategies), that one is essentially an acceptable person with many unique qualities and strengths? Where the therapist assumes the validity of the client, they also affirm and elicit it. Where there is no patronage, there is an equality in co-operation. As we will explore further in a later chapter, this also liberates the therapist and makes their work more joyful.

What does 'taking the client seriously' mean in practice? It means making some interesting assumptions.

- People's strategies relate in precise and intimate ways to their actual and anticipated life-experience.

What might be the positive reasons for someone to eat compulsively? Or split into multiple personalities? Or repeatedly seek out relationships in which they were undermined? There may, of course, be many reasons for each of these behaviours, some of which the client will recognise consciously even though they may not have realised the connection with the behaviour. For example, an elderly client with a compulsion for chocolate could describe her childhood with elderly, busy and often absent parents who gave her chocolate treats to keep her occupied, and her happy marriage to a diabetic who generously bought her the chocolate he could not eat himself, but without consciously connecting either with her current compulsion. Taking her daily consumption of 'family-sized' blocks of chocolate seriously opened up its elegantly relevant role in her life as a widow.

- Everyone does the best they can with the resources available to them.

If we accept the positive intent behind behaviour, it allows both client and therapist to move away from negative judgements. The caveat that behaviour relates to the choices the client has/had at the time allows us to locate limiting strategies at the level of behaviour rather than that of identity. The further assumption is that if a greater range of choices was available, the client would be able to make a more enabling choice. While it is easy to perceive the truth of this where the behaviour was framed in childhood (how appropriate for an abused child to learn to dissociate, or switch off from painful experiences and feelings), it is useful to assume that it remains true for behaviours framed in adulthood.

Therapy is then goal-directed: its aim, to enable the client to explore a greater range of choices which respect and address the same needs but in a less limiting, even more enabling way. The client with the passion for chocolate recognised and explored in a variety of ways her need for attention and love, for both short-term and longer-term 'sweetness' in her life, and began to take active steps to achieve it. Internal change and healing work went alongside very practical steps such as learning to be more assertive with her rather selfish and demanding son, making her daily life more pleasant by having her favourite armchair recovered and relocated in her window, so that she could easily enjoy watching the life of the street, and arranging to meet and phone her friends more often. As these new strategies began to take effect, her compulsion for chocolate waned and she began to lose weight, which in turn helped her to become more active.

- The client is the expert on themselves and their problem.

When we label a problem or condition, we run the serious risk of shifting our focus from the individual – this client with these behaviours and these feelings – to the class into which they appear to fit: 'the tumour in bed nine', 'the depressed teenager', the 'young woman with MPD'. Of course, categorisations have their uses, but there is an inbuilt risk, when we apply and use them, that we will begin to fit the client to the category – in other words, to reify the problem.

Clients who have seen other professionals before they come to us have often learnt to do this to themselves: they have added a de-individualising label to the difficulties they already had: 'The doctor told me I'm so disturbed I'm likely to become a long-stay mental patient', 'I've got bipolar affective disorder'. The client has been handed a description of their condition by an outside authority figure, the expert on the mind. If, like a recent client, they are themselves an expert on the mind, they can even do it to themselves, with similar effects: 'My childhood experience taught me learned helplessness.'

What happens if we assume that the client is the expert on them-self, with the fullest possible case history encoded in their own mind and body, with a highly specific knowledge of just what is wrong and what needs to change, and with the potential resources to bring about those changes? We find ourselves in a position of respectful curiosity; our work becomes the work of learning, experimentation, discovery; our explicit and implicit message to the client is that change is possible, within their power and their abilities; that they can and will be the architects of their own success, and that, like a consultant, we put ourselves at their service at every stage of the process from the recognition of the problem to its resolution. As the expert, they will be the one to know when enough has been done, or when a pause is required; when a task is helpful or overwhelming. As the expert, the client is right.

How does the therapist go about communicating this fundamental belief to the client? Sometimes, just by a brief and apparently 'throwaway' comment, for example when the client is expressing doubt about what their behaviour 'really means', or about what they should do next. 'You're the expert on you, so how does that seem to you?', or, 'You're the best judge of what's right for you, so what might help you to evaluate the possibilities now?' In each case, the structure of the sentence emphasises the question which forms its second part; but the important framing – and thus the underlying message to the client – is given in the statement with which it begins. The NLP therapist is also likely to be giving the same message by consistently referring to the client for verification: 'What will tell you that . . .?', 'How will you know . . .?', 'How does that feel . . .?' Such questions confirm to the client the therapist's assumption that the benchmark of what is happening is its impact upon the client: their feelings, their experience, their understanding, the choices open to them. This is a process of ongoing yet unobtrusive modelling, which helps the client learn to ask these same questions of themselves. As therapy progresses, the clients' own comments show how this self-reference is becoming increasingly habitual. Sometimes it may go through a somewhat self-conscious stage, in which the client says: 'I should be asking myself how I'll know, shouldn't I?' Usually, this is fairly brief: encouragement has been needed initially to put in place a process of self-referencing which rapidly feels natural because of its fundamental authenticity.

Another way in which therapists can convey this message enacts the principles of NLP in a different manner. We can communicate in many ways, both implicit and explicit, the message that the client has many choices, and that it is their choice, and their satisfaction with it, which tells them it is 'right'. A school refuser who visited an NLP therapist was carefully paced in his anxieties about entering a new school, and his therapist was particularly careful to put across, in a number of ways, that her role was not to persuade him but to help him become more resourceful in dealing with his fearful feelings, pressure from the educational system, mixed messages from his parents and his own wish to be able to get over the initial hurdle of going to the school and staying there.

After a number of gently paced sessions, the therapist reminded him that she was being paid to be his consultant (a role which he understood since his father used business consultants), and summarised the options he had. 'You have a place at the grammar school – and you know you'll enjoy it once you can get through the first day or so; you can continue to stay at home, and you have the option of going to a school for school refusers, where the teachers and the other kids will understand what you're going through. The downside of the grammar school is that they aren't very sympathetic to your difficulties; the difficulty about staying at home long-term is that you're going to get even more bored, quite apart from any pressures on you and your parents to make you go to school; and the disadvantage of the refusers' school is that while you are basically fine apart from this one difficulty, there will be kids there who have lots of problems and you may get labelled by being there. You've made your point about being messed about by your father's job changes, and I think you and your parents are now about equal. So you need to choose what's right for you.'

The client listened very intently and carefully, agreeing that he was indeed 'Ok apart from just this one problem'. The therapist had respected his self-knowledge and made it clear that in her view he had, even at 14, the ability to weigh up the advantages and disadvantages of the options open to him. A couple of weeks later the boy's mother reported that he had chosen the refusers' school, and that both staff and pupils had sensitively helped him overcome the initial entry. Six months later, a Christmas card reported that he was 'loving school' and doing well academically and at sport.

Emphasising the client's role as expert on themselves does not, of course, devalue our skills or our importance in the process of solving their difficulties. Experts need to call in independent evaluators sometimes, to ask for specialist help in suggesting what might be done and in what order, and to learn necessary skills. But regarding the client as the expert puts us firmly at their service – and relieves us of the burden of responsibility for them. Wendy still remembers a moment of immense relief early in her work as a therapist when it suddenly dawned on her that she was not responsible for her clients getting better: only they could do that. But the additional learning of NLP since then has added clarity to this felt experience. Similarly, Ian recalls the feeling of liberation that went with being able to say to a client's question, 'I don't know'. It is delightful and enabling to realise that there is no need for us to try to control the situation. If problems exist not in people's actual experience but in their structuring of it, then they alone have the information about how they do that (even if it is not presently in conscious awareness), and they alone can restructure it in ways which alleviate distress and make life more enjoyable and fulfilling. We cannot do that for them, but we can reliably offer assistance and co-create a system with them that makes this change possible.

● Each person knows best what their goals are.

If we assume that each of us has potentially as much of a blueprint for 'normal', 'healthy' emotional functioning as we do for physical, then that blueprint will guide us towards appropriate goals. Sometimes these may be clearly articulated at the outset of therapy: 'I want to be more in control of my eating'; 'I want to get on better with my wife'; 'I want to be able to make presentations confidently'; 'I want to let the past go'. Sometimes the client may need our help in shifting to an outcome frame. The effect can be dramatic, as Ian remembers:

C: I'm depressed.
Ian: So what do you want?
C: I don't really know.
Ian: And if you did know?
C: I'd be able to break free of mother, take control of my own life and do the art course I've always wanted to do.

Within NLP, we don't have to consider whether 'the client needs to stop going over and over the past', or, 'needs to take a more active role in standing up to his boss'. The client tells us what they need. Equally, if the client says they feel they no longer need therapy, we don't have to lament that 'there is really so much more they need to do', and feel obscurely guilty that somehow we haven't managed to convince them to 'finish it off'. Their satisfaction determines what enough is.

One client, for example, came for a number of sessions seeking help for lack of confidence. He was a well-respected university lecturer, caught up in a destructive personal relationship which he could not bring himself to end, and feeling very inadequate among his peers despite his professional skills and successes. He reached a point where he felt more confident and able to move forward, and decided to stop coming for therapy even though the relationship was still ongoing. Nine years later he phoned his therapist again: 'I don't know if you remember me: you really helped me about nine years ago. I have to make some important decisions, and I'd really value talking them through with you'. Both client and therapist knew that they had not fully 'worked through' all his initial concerns – nor did they need to. The client had been satisfied that he could manage his life better, had made a number of important changes (including, eventually, the ending of the traumatic relationship) and was now considering apparently unrelated life-decisions which would affect him, his family and his professional career. His reappearance confirmed that therapy had given him the help he wanted in the past, so he believed that he would again receive what he needed. This time, two sessions proved to be sufficient.

• The language in which we express ourselves is usually an exact encoding of our internal experience, and therefore, if carefully listened to, provides precise information which can guide the attentive therapist and suggest very specifically the changes that will make for improvement.

One of the major features of excellent and attentive therapists is their awareness of the client's language as a precise instrument for expressing the exact nature of their experience. From Freud's awareness of linguistic slips as an indicator of unconscious material, good therapists have consistently striven to 'hear' what the client is saying. In exploring and describing how people structure their internal experience, NLP has demonstrated how very exactly, and individually, we encode our experience in sensory terms, and how revealing our language is of how we do this.

The person who says that their responsibilities are a burden to them, that their heart is heavy, that what they need is somehow to become lighter and move forward, is telling us not just that they are overwhelmed and stuck, but *how* this experience is for them: it is kinesthetic. Another person may say that they 'simply can't see a way forward', their options are 'unclear', and that they need help in 'seeing it all from a different perspective'. This is quite different. They describe their experience in visual terms. Someone who says that the treatment they receive from their boss 'stinks' and that their colleagues 'really get up my nose' is telling us that, for them, the world currently offends their olfactory sense.

If as therapists we are attentive to the way in which these individual clients code their experiences, we can literally talk to them 'in their own language'. We can help the first client to 'find ways to move forward more freely', assist the second to 'get things into sharper focus', and enable the third to find what will make their life at work 'smell sweeter'. If, on the other hand, we respond without attentiveness to the language that shows us so exactly how the client represents the world to themselves, there is a danger that we may end up mismatching them. At its least intrusive, this means that the client will have to translate from our favoured system into theirs: they have to be flexible enough to deal with our inattentiveness. More disruptively, the mismatch may leave them feeling unheard, misunderstood or unvalued.

Another way in which clients give us important information about how they construct their experience of the world is through their use of metaphors and common phrases. NLP helps us to be acutely sensitive to language use, and leads us to take seriously even what appear to be 'dead metaphors'. For example, the woman who in the course of a single session says three or four times of her family that she 'loves them to death' is telling us more than that she loves them a lot. If we are attentive to her words, we will be asking ourselves how loving them might bring them, or her, or their relationship, 'to death'. We may choose to draw attention to the metaphor, discussing its meaning explicitly with her, or we may simply 'flag' it for ourselves and work with it more indirectly.

It is precisely the fact that some metaphors have through common use ceased to attract attention that allows the unconscious to select them: the metaphor both indicates and disguises the experience. As we develop our ability to pay exact and unfailing attention to clients, we find a wealth of information: they truly 'know more than they know they know', in Erickson's well-known phrase. Our attentiveness enables us to bring more of this knowledge to their service. Like many other processes, it can also help the client, through our modelling, to become more self-attentive: when we repeat back to the client something they have just said, any Rogerian reflecting has an extra dimension: if we are using the client's own words we are both validating their way of encoding their experience and also allowing them to hear the way they have encoded it. 'You love them to death . . .'. 'That's a strange thing for me to say, isn't it?' We would argue that this is one reason why the Rogerian approach works: the process of reflecting back using the client's own words provides them with a respectful, genuinely accepting context which truly allows them to perceive, in full awareness, what may have hitherto been largely unconscious. This is a very different route to insight from that offered by interpretation and external comments on behaviour.

Further, responding from within the client's system allows us to test if our understanding of them is correct. Where we repeat a metaphor that is genuinely 'dead', the client will usually make it clear that it is only a figure of speech: 'I don't really mean he's a stinker – but he's certainly irritating.' An attentive therapist might then check again: 'Just how does he irritate you?'

- The therapist is attentive to the client through their full range of sensory awareness.

Most therapeutic trainings emphasise the importance of 'listening skills', and as we have suggested, there are a number of layers of meaning in what the client tells us through speech. But good therapists have always used their other senses too, and NLP trainings develop our ability to gather information through the full range of senses. The underlying assumption is that mind and body are inextricably interconnected, and that therefore feelings *cannot not* be communicated somehow. Facial expression, body movement and stillness are at the grosser end of the scale: tiny changes in skin colour, muscle tone, orientation of the body in a number of directions and planes, gesturing with either or both hands and in particular directions, all provide us with subtler information, especially when related to what is being offered verbally.

In particular, the therapist's close attention to the timing of any changes cues them into possible significance. The client who gestures down towards her lap when expressing her wish to become her own person may be signalling non-verbally, too. However, the same gesture may have a number of personal meanings. Sometimes it may be appropriate to comment, or even to ask: other times, we can store the information and wait to see if the gesture happens again, and in what context. Next time around, we may get a reinforcement of one or another possible meaning. The client whose facial muscles suddenly lose tone and become flaccid when asked what he wants, at the same time as his body becomes still and his gaze fixed, is likely to have entered a naturalistic trance as he seeks inside for the answer to the question, and we can notice this and not make the mistake of inadvertently interrupting his flow by talking prematurely.

Such ongoing changes provide the attentive therapist with a delightfully precise running commentary on the overt work of the therapy, and when the client learns to run a similar kind of simul-taneous self-monitoring they too can find their self-understanding much enhanced. 'When you asked me to consider that, I felt myself draw back, as though it was too hard at the moment.' In becoming self-aware to this extent, this client has learnt to tap into their own unconscious responses, and we can usually take their immediate interpretations at face value: tone, speed of response and degree of conviction are all very different from those of an over-intellectualis-ing or compliant client attempting to 'analyse' their motivation. Where the second kind of response is like a critical commentary, the first comes across more as an attempt at spontaneous translation.

The client's words, in turn, prescribe appropriate interventions: 'So even *thinking* about thinking about that felt too hard just yet?', 'So there might be another moment, but not yet, when it wouldn't be too hard?', 'What might you need, do you feel, that would help it not be too hard?', 'If there were something that made it less hard, might it be the right moment?'

Another important range of information which NLP has given us concerns eye-accessing cues, and some common patterns have been noted in the Eye Accessing Cues Schematic. As with any schematic representation it is a simplification. There are many interesting anomalies. Nonetheless, the schematic can be useful in attracting and directing our attention to an important range of information, offered unconsciously by the client.

When you talk with a client, you may notice how their eye-movements appear to accompany internal processing. A lot is going on. Simply noticing this class of behaviour, and how it relates to the individual client, will make you more observant. If you notice that a particular client looks upwards, squints, then says, 'I can't see a way through', or, 'It's not at all clear to me', you may get curious about just what they're doing on the inside before uttering those words. You might, for instance, hypothesise that they were involved in some visual processing that it was not possible to complete satisfactorily, and which gave rise to the words that followed. This is a testable hypothesis if you choose to ask the client what they were doing inside.

Here, it is important to differentiate between process and content. Ian frequently demonstrates these accessing patterns in practitioner trainings. On one occasion he asked a man who loved classical music to hear again the opening bars of Beethoven's 5th Symphony. The man looked up to his left (V^r), then his eyes went to the mid-line and left (A^r). When Ian asked the group what the man was doing there were many explanations – he was reading the score, then hearing the music, or seeing the orchestra playing, then hearing the music. There

Eye-movements are unconscious, and therefore a source of potentially valuable additional information about what is going on for the client. Often, as in this case, they occur in significant and repeated sequences.

A client was berating herself for being self-destructive: she knew she would feel better if she got her accounts in order, yet kept putting it off. Wendy noted that as the client described her feelings of resentment and disappointment, she kept looking down to her right. When asked to imagine completing the work, the client first looked up to her right, then down to her right. Her expression was first one of curiosity, with a slight smile, then she pursed her lips and frowned as she looked down again. Asked what she had been experiencing as she did this, the client said that though she could see herself doing the work, and knew she would feel better for it, in fact she had felt cross and unhappy. She was asked to repeat the process to check it, and this time as she looked down her face suddenly looked more child-like. Noticing this, Wendy asked whether it was the grown-up who felt cross at the idea of doing the work, or perhaps a younger self. The client then said that though the grown-up wanted to do the work and knew she would feel better, 'little me' didn't want to do it because if she didn't, people would realise that she was unhappy. The client commented that as a child she had avoided doing all her schoolwork in one subject entirely for three years in the hope that people would wonder why.

As this example shows, the sequence of eye-movements first accompanied and was then used to help reveal complex internal processing. The therapist's sensory acuity allowed her to note the sequence of movements, and to connect with it the changes in facial expression and tone that happened as the client connected with her past experiences.

Another client, who often used such phrases as 'I'm always telling myself . . .', 'I remind myself that . . .', used at the same time to look down and to his left. Since the conjunction of the language with that particular eye-movement seemed to indicate that internal dialogue was going on, Ian was able to match the preferred form of internal processing by suggesting to the client that 'you might explain to yourself that . . .' or 'ask yourself if . . .'.

Eye-accessing cues are taught as part of the practitioner training, and trainees learn to register them as part of the range of information the client is making available. This not only adds to our understanding of how the client is constructing their subjective experience, but also enables us to help the client make the changes they desire in the most effective, because most individually tailored and appropriate, way. If the difficulty is structured in pictures, changing the pictures changes the problem. If the problem is a felt one, changing the kinesthetic experience changes the way it feels.

In our opinion, the therapeutic value of working with eye-movements has yet to be fully recognised. Recently, though, it has been demonstrated again in the painless and rapid results achievable using Eye Movement Densitisation Routine (EMDR).

Often, the client may habitually run a sequence involving more than one 'representational system'. And again, the attentive curiosity of the therapist is a primary means of helping the client to become aware of their own processing, so that they can develop skills for developmental change. Learning which initially happens in the context of a problem has applications far beyond the therapeutic encounter: it becomes a truly generative, permanent life-tool. The client who had found difficulty with her paperwork, for example, reported that as she lay in bed in the morning, reluctant to get up and start the day, she had pictured herself finishing the chores she needed to do around the house and being able to go to work with a clear conscience, and that having checked that this would indeed feel good (using the up–right then down–right sequence she had first experienced in therapy), she found herself getting up instead of day-dreaming as she often did.

Where this degree of attention is paid to the client, the possibility of misunderstanding is greatly reduced. We are guided by a greater range of information, much of which, because unconscious and involuntary, is more reliable. We are therefore in a position to notice and check out inconsistencies and incongruities – mismatches, in NLP terms, between what is said and what is actually experienced. This goes beyond the crude, and actually rather infrequent situation, in which a client might knowingly seek to present partial or skewed information. Incongruities at this level are much more likely to be between what the client consciously thinks they feel and what they know at an unconscious level. For example, someone who responds to the question, 'Do you enjoy your work?' with a 'Yes', while at the same time their head makes a minute, side-to-side 'no' movement.

At another level, we can check out the effectiveness of our interventions by being very attentive to the client's responses. This can be particularly helpful in the case of dutiful or compliant clients, who may genuinely want an intervention to work and feel that its lack of, or partial, effectiveness is somehow their fault. In these circumstances, they are unlikely to express their disappointment, but the therapist can notice and reflect back small but crucial physiological indicators, 'You frowned a little there. How come?' Such accepting and detailed observation is, of course, also instrumental in enhancing rapport, and can become an important means of modelling to the client an acceptance of their own doubts and reservations. As with so much in NLP, the learning can go far beyond the immediate situation, and the client can acquire through it enabling skills for intra-psychic work of their own.

The role of pacing and leading

NLP suggests that pacing and leading are at the heart of any successful communication. Pacing, which involves the sensitive modelling of the client's verbal and non-verbal behaviour and thus a joining with them in their way of constructing experience, goes far beyond an attempt to copy the client. Mimicry, a crude imitation of observable behaviour, alienates and renders the other self-conscious. Effective communicators, on the other hand, demonstrate a sensitive and flexible ability to enter the world of the person they are communicating with – whether this be in the context of therapy, teaching, business or personal relationships – and to demonstrate this imperceptibly to the other through their matching of many subtle as well as obvious features of the other's behaviour and speech. Everyday phrases suggest part of what is needed to do this: 'stepping into someone else's shoes'; 'seeing the world through their eyes'; 'getting in touch'; 'being in tune'.

At its best, though, this is much more. It is the co-creation of a system. It is a process in which the therapist co-explores with the client the client's way of being; one where the therapist co-creates a space where both can engage with, deconstruct and reconstruct the client's map of the world, limiting behaviours, capabilities and beliefs and ultimately the client's very sense of self, their identity.

Where there is pacing, there can be leading. In a children's book written in the 50s, the author Monica Edwards (1966 [1952], pp. 203–6) describes how one of the young heroes is having a nightmare, and talking in his sleep. One of the friends with whom he is staying wakes, and rather than waking him first listens carefully, then quietly begins to add small comments, then longer sentences, to make the dreamer's speech into a conversation. The dreamer's state is not rudely broken, but the friend's quiet and gradual intervention develops until he is eventually led from his anxiety to a state of calmness, all without waking. This is pacing and leading.

The underlying assumption is that if we are prepared to join the other person in their mapping of the world, we are accorded – by them – the privilege of influencing them. Further, the respectfulness of this process often provides them with a model by which they may begin to influence themselves.

We can pace and lead very effectively at many different levels. Let's look at an example. A female executive client arrives half an hour late for an appointment, having been delayed by an accident that caused a traffic-jam. She is agitated, irritated, talking quickly and sitting restlessly. The practitioner matches her, acknowledging this frustration both verbally and behaviourally. He makes sure that he too is talking somewhat faster and sitting towards the edge of his chair rather than adopting a 'laid-back' position. Then he says, changing tone and pace, 'So how can we make the *best use* of *the time we do have?*' and the client is then able to focus in on what she really wants to get out of the session.

Another example concerns a father who was finding it really difficult to be patient with his small child, Sam. Every morning there was a row when it came to getting the child up for school: the father would attempt to wake him, Sam would be sleepy, he would give him an ultimatum, Sam would fall asleep again. Though they mostly got to school on time the day had begun badly. The counsellor explained the value of pacing before attempting to lead, and suggested that the father should go into Sam's room a few minutes earlier in the morning, lie down beside him, wake him from this prone position and just talk with him about the day ahead. After a few moments he could remind Sam that he must be beginning to feel hungry now after so many hours, and that breakfast was waiting downstairs. From the initial pacing of his sleepiness, the father was able to lead his son and without nagging or ultimatums, into a more wakeful state and then towards actually wanting to get up. After this had happened a few times, Sam started to become alert more rapidly on being roused: his father's initial pacing and then leading had given him an opportunity of associating waking up with special time for just him and his dad, so that he could then begin to initiate the process himself.

In summary, the core of therapeutic work in NLP rests on the establishment of a relationship of respectful mutual attentiveness between the client and therapist. The core of the work is the problem, as the client defines it: the success of the therapy is the resolution of the problem in terms acceptable to the client and the therapist; the process of the collaborative work is one which respects the individuality of both partners, and which thereby models to the client their own resourcefulness and ability to take charge of their own life.

Conceptual model: calibrated loops

We are all familiar with the notion of vicious circles, and of their beneficial counterpart, analeptic or virtuous circles. In NLP the term *loops* is used to identify repeating sequences involving internal or external behaviours, or a mixture of both. *Calibration* is the process of attending to and drawing conclusions from changes across a full range of available information – for example, noticing changes in posture, muscle tone or skin colour that provide information on someone's experience in parallel to what they are overtly doing or saying.

A 'calibrated loop' is a complex sequence of events which can involve more than one person and which, like a computer programme, is repeated over and over again. Its elements and sequence can be identified, and operate as a complex series of rules, involving thought, emotion, behaviour in both (or all) parties. Work and family relationships provide many examples of these – both virtuous and vicious in outcome. Wendy taught for a number of years as part of a course-team responsible for a teacher-training course: the team involved seven people working closely together, and she became aware that its meetings developed a routine sequence, repeating the same kinds of discussions, arguments and interactions. In a mixture of amusement and frustration, one day she eventually wrote out a set of behavioural 'Rules for Team Meetings' on the model of the printed instructions sold with table games. One rule even specified that if a certain move was made (specifically, if one of a number of key trigger words was said by any party), the four predictable interchanges which followed would be 'deemed to have taken place'. When she showed these 'rules' to colleagues, they laughed – while wryly admitting their accuracy.

The concept of calibrated loops has much to offer both clients and therapists. It can help us disentangle the kind of intimate downward spiralling which often begins with some innocuous event or remark and leads rapidly and apparently unavoidably to harsh words and the slamming of doors – a process which Eric Berne in *Games People Play*, named 'Uproar' (1969; p. 114). Equally, it can help us work out how certain kinds of encounters can reliably succeed – a beneficial calibrated loop is likely to be involved. The assumption is that each party to the interaction is consciously and unconsciously calibrating, that is to say, paying attention to the other at many levels, and that each response relates to what is understood by its predecessor – and then acts as stimulus to how the other party reacts in their turn.

As therapists, it can be useful to consider what kinds of calibrated loops are involved between us and our clients. If we know more about the effective loops, we are in a position to re-create what works (to model it, in fact). If we know more about what works less well (why work is 'harder' or 'makes less progress' or we 'feel less confident' with certain clients), we are better able to interrupt the pattern, to make it explicit and therefore an overt part of the work where appropriate, or to identify where our own material may be being triggered by the client and to deal with it outside the therapy room.

Often, it's finding the trigger points that gives us new insight and new leverage. The list of rules Wendy made showed how certain interchanges were 'set off' by the use of key words, which triggered repeating, unresolvable, ideological arguments among the team. Sometimes it may be a certain look, or a gesture. One client's father had manipulatively abused her as a child, first offering, then withdrawing, sexual contact. When in adult life she noticed that a man seemed first to be attracted to her but then lost interest, she became childlike in her desperation at being rejected, anxious to 'sort things out' with him, and finally angry at his failure to understand what she was feeling. Often her behaviour was inappropriate to her adult self, and to the here-and-now situation. Where once the client believed that the whole sequence and its unpleasant and embarrassing outcomes were 'inevitable', she found that the key trigger to the dénouement of this calibrated loop was being told by the man to 'go away' or 'leave'. Her therapist helped her to break down the sequence into a number of stages, exploring each to discover where she could make different choices and exit from the programme before it reached its final point.

Client–therapist system Skill-builders

Therapist
- Take three professional helpers you have personally encountered, two whom you have found helpful and one whom you have found limited or less helpful. In what ways are you currently modelling the helpful behaviour? Could you usefully model it more? In what ways are you avoiding the less desirable behaviour?
- Ask yourself what would you ideally like to add into your therapist–client system (for example, humour, a more educational or self-help emphasis)?

Supervisor
- Consider the kind of relationship you are encouraging your supervisees to build with their clients. In how many ways are you currently modelling that kind of relationship to them, and what else might you be able to add? Examine, for example:
  - the collaborative element;
  - the quality of the rapport;
  - the degree of pacing.

Client–therapist system Transformer

Be your client
Imagine being one of your own clients.

- What's it like meeting up with you?
- What's it like working with you?
- What relationship is presupposed when encountering you?

Include all of the following:

- advertising material;
- answer machine message;
- first telephone conversation;
- conventions about how you name each other;
- the layout of the furniture in your house/office;
- meeting and greeting, including waiting area and refreshments (or absence of);
- therapy room;
- form of case-taking procedure;
- note-taking;
- opening questions about therapeutic aim or issue;
- home-work or tasks;
- the ending of the session;
- payment and arrangements about future appointments;
- cancellation procedures.

Are there any changes you would wish to make?

Part 2
NLP: Working in Partnership

6
NLP Benefits to the Client

I am often asked about my psychotherapeutic method. I cannot reply unequivocally to the question. Therapy is different in every case. When a doctor tells me that he adheres strictly to this or that method, I have my doubts about his therapeutic effect. So much is said in the literature about the resistance of the patient that it would almost seem as if the doctor were trying to put something over on him, whereas the cure ought to grow naturally out of the patient himself . . . I treat every patient as individually as possible, because the solution of the problem is always an individual one.

(Carl Jung, *Memories, Dreams, Reflections*, 1977: 152)

In the previous chapter we looked at the nature of the relationship between client and therapist as a systemic process involving mutual attentiveness, in which the basic assumptions are that the client is their own best diagnostician, and will let us know precisely not only what is wrong, but what needs to happen to fix it.

This chapter offers some answers to the question: 'What are the distinctive benefits to the client of NLP therapy?' Since it is our belief that the messages are those which the client actually receives, we have chosen to frame them as they might be heard/felt/seen by the client, regardless of whether they were explicitly or implicitly articulated in the process of the therapy.

Here is a perfect place to start from

Clients usually come to therapy with negative feelings about them-selves. These self-judgements may be either generalised or applied to specific behaviours. They truly feel they are not in the right place, but may also assume on the basis of previous experience or ideas about what therapy entails that change takes place as the result of more or less lengthy preparatory processes.

One client, for example, had been in weekly therapy for a number of years, exploring difficult and painful childhood experiences which he could relate to his current adult depression and professional underachievement, but felt he had reached an impasse. His assumption in the previous therapy had been that this exploratory and uncovering work was needed before change could take place: that, in other words, he could not just begin from where he was. He was pleasantly surprised to discover that he could learn how to change the structure and sequencing of his habitual thinking in ways that had immediate and significant effects. Serious work, could, after all, begin immediately.

It is not even necessary to have a clearly articulated sense of what is wrong, or of what the goal is. Another client felt very confused, aware that he was apparently functioning appropriately in his role as a schoolteacher, but also experiencing a sense of distance and anxiety. It was acknowledged that he did not have to have a clear definition of his 'problem' – but how would he know when things improved? By feeling less distant and less anxious, of course. Exploration of exactly how he structured those feelings, and how he structured his experience at those times when it was different and he was more comfortable with himself, started a process of learning and change at a profound and influential level.

Nothing is taken away

Because NLP assumes that all behaviour has positive intent, the client is encouraged to experience how it feels to accept, and wonder about, all the aspects of the self which have been involved in problem behaviour. NLP allows the client to identify and value the purposefulness of even bizarre or self-destructive behaviour, while at the same time aiding the development of additional choices. One client had learnt early in her life to accommodate both her demanding mother and sister and her much-loved but also dominant father. In adult life she perpetuated this pattern: quick to sympathise with others' problems, she was often taken advantage of. Recognising the way in which she structured her experience, and the benefits it brought her, allowed her to find ways to express her caring while making choices of friends and partners who did not exploit or seek to dominate her.

Another client, whose extreme childhood trauma had led her to split into multiple personalities, learnt to accept that this was the nature of her coping strategy, that each part had valuable and benevolent intent, and was consequently able to develop ways of working creatively and more effectively with the divisions. She was adamant that she did not wish to 'integrate' the parts, which she felt would involve major loss; and this caveat was accepted as the basis for the therapy. She recognised, for example, the usefulness of a sub-personality who could ensure that she kept appointments, another who would bear pain but then retreat so that she could detach from it, and even of one – the child who had been involved in the most traumatic of the childhood experiences – who would come to the therapy sessions and hide behind a spare chair. While no direct communication was possible between this personality and either the various other selves or the therapist, it was crucial that she was willing to be present, and known to be so. This particular therapy was long-term, but the nature of the assumptions about the client, and the messages she received, were no different than those involved in short-term work. After years of medication, alcoholism and drug-dependence, during which various forms of therapy, including hospitalisation, had failed to establish a basis for improvement, the client was eventually able to sustain her sobriety, to form a successful relationship and to undertake retraining prior to seeking employment again.

I get to realise I'm not a second-class citizen

Many clients have learnt to think of themselves as inferior, either because they were told so or because they too believe their behaviour to be flawed. It is in keeping with the NLP assumption that people are making the best choices they can, that clients receive a clearly different message, which while acknowledging their difficulties, respects their equality as individuals. For some, this can raise taxing and potentially threatening conflicts with their belief structure. One client who came seeking help for depression after a relationship break-up was a member of AA, and had not drunk alcohol for over eight years. She was well liked and respected within the Fellowship, firmly believed that her own rehabilitation had been due to AA and had been invited by a number of other members to be their sponsor, mentoring their own process of rehabilitation.

As she became more self-valuing and less depressed, finding both employment after a long absence from work and a promising new relationship, she noticed that she was becoming uneasy in AA meetings. Exploring this, she realised that her anxiety was raised only in meetings in her home town, which involved many newish members in crisis, but not in meetings she attended in other towns, where the membership had been longer in recovery and where the emphasis was more on the purposeful living of life.

This raised a dangerous question for her: she began to feel that her *fit* within AA had 'some rough edges to it'. While she understood AA's requirement that its members continually acknowledge their alcoholism – 'I am X, and I'm an alcoholic' – she felt as though she was 'having the word on my forehead – as though I'm looking through glass on which it's painted, so I have to see the world through it. I know now I'm not second-class, but this says I'm different.' She felt she would like to move the word somewhere less obtrusive (her gestures placed it at shoulder level), while continuing to own it, but was fearful that if she did so she would be complacent and forget its message, and that this might mean she would drink again.

It was critical that the therapist stayed within the client's belief structure and did not in any way cause her to doubt it, while at the same time respecting that she needed to find a new and more forward-looking way to relate to the beliefs that had saved her. Careful pacing of feelings, beliefs and sub-modality organisation supported the client until she herself found her solution: 'AA also talks a lot about "recovery"', she said. 'Maybe I just need to add the word *recovering* to the label I'm looking through.' Asked how that felt, she said it felt fine: she would eventually like to move the phrase from her forehead, but if it turned out to be too dangerous to shift the label to a less obtrusive location she would still be much happier to look at the world through the phrase '*recovering* alcoholic'. As a start, she would just amplify the label.

Once we start working with NLP it gets hard to maintain the myth that 'I'm a victim'

Carl Rogers, among others, pointed out in his book *On Becoming a Person* (1967), how one of the major indicators of progress in therapy is that the client ceases to blame circumstances or others for their situation and begins to move from this essentially passive position to one where they take an active responsibility for moving things on. This may sometimes involve recognising that they have played a part in creating or maintaining dysfunctional patterns; but even where they may clearly have been a blameless victim the same process may occur. It is as though the client somehow reached the decision 'Even though what happened was unfair/unjust/damaging, even though I was not to blame, I can now do something about it'. The client moves from a victim role to a proactive role in their own life.

NLP helps the client make this transition faster and more easily than many investigative forms of therapy, because from the beginning of the very first session the client will be addressed as the expert: the one who knows about their problem, the one who has the right to determine their own goals; the one who possesses, even if unconsciously, all the resources that are needed to make the desired changes.

One client illustrated how this process can sometimes usefully disrupt old patterns. She felt she had been misunderstood and undervalued by her parents following the death in a road accident of an older sister, whom they had idolised and to whom they had compared her unfavourably. The dead child had been the 'little princess', the living one was a tomboy. As a teenager, she joined the armed forces, and after working her time she became a security officer, all the while both trying to please her parents and actively resenting them. There were many quarrels and tensions, and she felt helpless to influence the relationship for the better. When she came for therapy, in her 30s, she began by describing and attacking her parents' unreasonable attitudes and behaviour – which were objectively evidenced by letters they had sent her which she showed to the therapist. While respecting and pacing her anger and sense of having been undervalued, the therapist helped her to focus on what kind of relationship she really wanted with her parents, and to develop strategies that would help her assert her grown-up self when she interacted with them. The work continued for a number of months, during which the client realised that she no longer felt a victim, but could begin to determine how she wanted to be treated. As a result of her new-found clarity and self-confidence, she stopped trying to placate her parents and began to resent them less; and when some years later she brought her partner along for help for a different issue, she was able to say that her contact with her parents was more equal and equitable.

We work with *my* goal

Often, the first question the client is asked in NLP therapy is a version of 'What do you want?' The message is that they are the ones with the right to decide what they want to achieve through the process of working with us. An NLP therapist does not need to make assumptions about what the client 'really needs' to do. The client is assumed to be the expert on what they want. Sometimes, as we showed earlier, they will be helped to reformulate their goal in such a way as to make it more achievable; sometimes, the therapist will help the client chunk up to explore what the desired goal will itself help them achieve, so revealing it to be a subset of something yet more significant; but the goal itself will be accepted at face value.

These two additional processes work with the client's agenda to ensure that its aims can be fulfilled. If a client's goal, for example, is that another person changes their mind, or their behaviour, the client can be helped to realise that because this is not within their control, the goal itself is compromised. If the goal is unrealistic in that it requires greater investment of time or other resources than the client is able or willing to make, they can be helped to realise that this also compromises their probable success. On other occasions, it may be helpful to explore how the overt goal will lead to some other goal –

usually a more fundamental one, but sometimes one which the client has not consciously recognised. A process of respectful questioning by the therapist – 'and what will that achieve for you?' – may lead, perhaps through a series of stages, from a very specific aim, to a much wider, all-embracing one:

> *Client:* I want to become more confident so that I can pass my driving test.
> *Therapist:* And what will that do for you?
> *Client:* I will be able to drive myself where I want to go.
> *Therapist:* And how will that help you?
> *Client:* I will be able to go to evening classes without depending on my husband.
> *Therapist:* And that means . . .?
> *Client:* That I will be less controlled by my husband.
> *Therapist:* And when you are . . .?
> *Client:* Then I will be more in control of my own life.

The therapist asked for more information in order to understand within the client's map of the world why the driving test was significant. In the process, the client became very clear. However, becoming confident so as to be able to pass the driving test still retained its importance. Now, though, both knew just how important it was and why.

Where we take the client's goal as the legitimate aim of therapy, we can often help them achieve it elegantly and rapidly. We do not need to get bogged down in a mass of other potential material.

A middle-aged woman asked for help with her agoraphobia, which was gradually restricting her life. She wanted to be able to visit the town centre to shop, and to take her elderly mother to the hair-dresser's without panicking. She had saved up enough housekeeping money for four sessions, which she insisted on paying for in advance. Almost in passing, she revealed that she and her sister had been abused by their father, and that her relationship with her elderly mother was complicated not only by her mother's current demand-ingness, but also by her previous failure to protect her daughters from the abuse. There was plenty of material that could have been 'worked on'! Given the client's clarity about her goal, and the restricted time-frame, therapy focused on how she would need to feel in order to leave the house and get to the places she wanted: in other words, on the recognition and effective management of physical, mental and emotional states. When she left after the third session, she forgot her spectacles. About an hour later she phoned and asked if it would be convenient for her to collect them. Instead of being driven by her husband, she arrived on foot, having taken a bus through the centre of the town at rush hour, followed by a brief walk through the streets from the bus-stop. She never came for her fourth session, but told the therapist to keep the money in case she ever needed another session. In 19 years that need has not arisen, and from time to time we've heard via a third party that the client is still enjoying a full and active life.

Once is enough

NLP focuses on the active recognition and change of patterns of self-organisation, rather than upon the detailed exploration of past events and the search for insight into them. Alongside this focus is the crucial assumption that the client has already suffered, and that the therapy should not – and does not need to – reiterate this. *To reiterate is not simply to do again: it is to risk reinforcing, retraumatising, enhancing those very feelings and learnings which the client seeks to heal and move away from.* As we have also shown, many clients come expecting this as an essential part of the therapy: the tooth must be drilled before it can be filled.

One client had received sustained counselling at work for some time before her welfare officer recommended she seek psychotherapy. At the client's request, the welfare officer gave the therapist a brief outline of the events of the client's life to date: her father had left her mother when she was a year old; the mother had remarried, and both she and the stepfather had favoured her elder sister and their joint child, a younger boy, consistently showing extreme interest in them and their progress while putting the client down and ignoring her achievements. At the riding stable where she had lessons in exchange for labour, she was abused by two different men. In her early 20s, her elder sister suddenly committed suicide: there had been no warning of this, although it afterwards emerged that she had been seeing a psychiatrist. The client was told by her mother that her sister's secret depression and suicide must have been caused by their birth-father's desertion (the sister had been four at the time). She believed that she was responsible for his desertion because he had probably been unable to put up with another baby in the house. For this and other reasons, she decided to trace her birth-father, a decision in which she was supported by her boyfriend (whom she later married), and to which her mother and stepfather initially agreed. However, once she had traced him and met with him more than once, her mother and stepfather disowned her, even refusing to attend her wedding.

The first session of therapy established that the client felt she could work with this second therapist; that she had learnt to switch off her feelings because they were so painful, and that she had an extremely low sense of self-esteem. In the second session, the client asked if it would be all right to stay for an hour rather than the therapist's normal one and a half hours, as she expected to be exhausted. The therapist said that the one and a half hour session was reserved for her, and that she could use as much or as little of it as she wanted. The client's demeanour changed dramatically when the therapist went on to say that, in her view, it was important to work with what the client wanted to achieve rather than yet again going over all these painful and sad experiences: 'Once is enough'. Though the client had said 'you will have to draw information out of me', she in fact went on to volunteer a considerable amount of information covering a range of experiences and feelings, and at times became quite lively and animated. At the end of the session she said quite clearly that she wanted to work first to build her confidence: she believed that once this was stronger, she would find it easier to deal with some of the past traumas which she did feel were in need of 'sorting'.

This example raises an important point: in our view the process of dissociation from painful experience, or closing it down through 'forgetting', is a natural and often entirely appropriate response, although, like all decisions, it can be limiting or have limiting and unforeseen consequences. If, as therapists, we respect that our clients may have dissociated from trauma as the result of unconscious choice, we will be less inclined to retraumatise them by getting them to relive their painful experiences and memories. This does not mean avoiding old traumas entirely: it means respecting the timing which is appropriate for the client rather than imposing our own. There will be many people who, like this client, feel the need to build their strength before they can tackle old injuries or even current wounds. Reminding ourselves that 'once is enough' helps us to focus on strengthening the client's resourcefulness, and puts them in the driving seat of the work we do together.

Where it is necessary to access painful or unpleasant experiences, NLP can call upon a number of techniques that allow clients to find information and to change limited learnings without reliving the original experiences in full. Events are experienced through our five senses; and they are subsequently coded internally through those same five senses. Careful exploration with the client prior to revisiting a powerful or traumatic event in the past – even in the apparently obvious one of asking the client to tell the therapist about it – will give the therapist specific information which can be used to make the 'visit' a protected one. Telling the story, as we often find in everyday life, is one way of reliving an experience; and for this reason the traditional therapeutic exploration of old events is likely to reinforce their emotional impact and ingrain whatever the client may have learnt from them – learnings which may well be part of the very 'problem' the client wants to change.

If we are seeking to help a client deal with a difficult, even traumatic, experience in order to help them recode its significance, lessen its trauma, or open up future choices in relation to what they learnt from it, we can co-create safe structures which allow engagement but at an appropriate and safe distance. For instance, we can invite them to view the event as if on a screen, while imagining themselves to be located in the comfortable, and controlling, position of a film projectionist. If needed, further 'layers' of protection might be added: from the safety of the projection booth they might watch themselves sitting in the seats below watching the movie of the event. We can use the video metaphor and give them pause, fast forward, rewind and edit buttons. Further protection from retraumatising can be achieved by changing the sub-modalities of its visual coding – for example, by watching the movie in black-and-white or at a greater distance.

Another powerful NLP approach which helps clients not only to work on their past but to begin to create a desired future involves working with a client's 'time-line'. Based on the discovery that virtually everyone codes their experience of time in a spatial and linear way, and that there are a number of common patternings, the therapist can help the client to work with their own Time Line in ways which can maintain a degree of distance, while allowing access to information and ways to incorporate more recent understandings and resources into archaic and limiting coding. However, Time Lines can also be used to help clients reconnect with their experience if they are disconnected from it. Either way, it is a significant experience in NLP that change does not only come *after* the therapy but *during* it. When dealing with past harm, we want the client to know without question that *it can be different now* – not just next week, or next month, but while they are with us in the session itself.

I get a sense of wonder and renewal of curiosity about myself and others

Because NLP teaches us to be alert to the structure of our subjective experience, it usually leads us to a wondering awareness of how miraculous we are. As we explore precisely how we do apparently ordinary everyday things, we can begin to marvel at the infinite variety and flexibility of the human brain. This applies to 'bad' things as well as 'good': how is it that we manage to have a panic attack not just when we fly in a plane but every time we even think about travelling by air? What do we do inside that helps us stay calm when we deal with irate customers on the telephone day in, day out? It is the act of becoming curious about the highly individual way in which we go about things that brings our own processing from out of awareness to become the focus of our attention – and thereby, of our wonder.

By extension, we become curious about how others structure their experience too: our families, our friends and colleagues. Do they do it like we do – or very differently? A recent dinner-party conversation brought up the subject of playing solitaire on the computer. It became apparent in this initially casual conversation that each of the people present had different strategies for playing the game, and as they compared notes they began to realise that the reality was far from their original assumption that people 'just play'. While this might initially appear a trivial example, it highlighted for these friends something they had not previously recognised about the subtlety and individuality of individual processing, and they began to consider what implications this might have for the way they handled decision-making in other areas of their lives, both personal and professional.

When we pay this kind of attention to the individual structuring of experience, we also begin to marvel at the human ability to learn new strategies, to deconstruct what previously seemed fixed, inevitable, limiting, and to reconstruct sequences that may be different in only small ways, yet can also have very different results. This can give a quite new dimension to what clients bring to the session.

A promising young athlete came for help because she had started to have problems with her take-off in the high jump. As the therapist asked her to describe in detail exactly what was going on for her when she prepared for a jump, and how this differed from times when take-off was not a problem, the athlete came to realise that the difficulty occurred only when she thought the bar had been set above a certain height. In this case, she then began to tell herself as she approached that it was too difficult, and that she would be bound to knock it down. This then broke the fluency of her approach, and she usually did end up knocking the bar. Her trainer, however, was convinced that she had not yet reached the limit of her potential.

To check experientially that the difficulties were in fact attributable to her doubting internal dialogue, the therapist suggested that the trainer be asked, at the next training session, to vary the height of the bar both up and down, not letting the athlete know the height: she for her part was to look the other way as the bar was adjusted, so that she would not be able to see if it was being raised or lowered. She was, however, to write down her estimate of the set height on each occasion. The next time the client came, she reported that she had experienced no difficulties in take-off, that her ability to estimate the actual bar height was very unreliable, and that she had on three occasions cleared more than her previous personal best. The client had become very curious about the role her self-talk was playing in her performance, and this was explored in more detail, so that limiting messages which she was still carrying over from the past could be modified. Since she now knew that these were creating the take-off problems, and that her actual potential as a jumper was greater than she had previously thought, she found that she was once again able to take off fluently, and went on to perform outstandingly at her next competition even though the bar-height was raised progressively and she knew on each occasion what it was. Her estimate of her 'personal ceiling' had been deconstructed, and she was now eager to continue exploring what she might be able to achieve. Her trainer was also fascinated, and began to consider with some of the other athletes he coached the impact of their personal beliefs and internal dialogue.

I can stop being reactive and begin to be proactive

For example, one client came for help with anxiety in riding her horse. She was frightened of hacking him out in traffic, and also became very anxious when competing, to the point where their performance was adversely affected. As she learnt to identify the precise ways in which she constructed her anticipatory anxiety, and began to develop new internal sequences that defused the situation, she also became curious about how she could develop strategies for improving her performance. Like many clients, she had shifted from an initial *away-from* motivation to a *towards*. Her original aims were both achieved: she became confident in riding out and was so much more relaxed in competition that she won for the first time. However, she also began to explore different NLP strategies which could help her refine her riding and her communication with her horse in a variety of ways, recognising that concepts like pacing and leading, for example, could have an inter-species value as well as an interpersonal one. As a result of this work, her trainer also became interested: skills initially learnt in a therapeutic context spread to the stable and the manège.

I get to know how my brain works

As we begin to consider our own experience with the kind of accepting attentiveness which NLP cultivates, we begin not only to marvel at the amazing versatility of our own minds, but to understand what is unique to the way each of us personally operates. This allows us to recognise and appreciate, perhaps for the first time, what we do really well (now knowing exactly how we go about it), and also to understand how we structure negative experiences – and what the differences are. This is empowering in its outcomes, but the deeper implication is that we can value, learn from and interact with our own uniqueness.

A university student was becoming very stressed in the revision period leading up to her final examinations. Asked to explore how she did being stressed, she said that she kept reminding herself of how much there was to learn and how little time there was. Further, she envisioned getting to the end of the revision period knowing she had not done enough. She spontaneously commented that 'The exams aren't the problem – you just do them. If you know what they're asking about, that's fine: if you don't, you do something with it anyway.' This recognition focused her on wondering just how she was organising these experiences differently from the way she had previously managed similar revision work involved in writing an assessed third-year placement project. She concluded that though the project also involved covering a mass of material before a specific deadline, she had just taken each day as it came, worked a bit, respected feelings of boredom and tiredness, taken breaks and then followed her own sense of readiness to pick up the work again.

In exploring these similar experiences with their very different results in this detailed and self-reflexive way, the student had taken herself through a process which NLP calls 'contrastive analysis': by means of comparing in this very specific way all stages of the process as she herself had internally organised and experienced it, she had found where the critical differences were. Her conclusion was that she should now run the rest of her finals revision in the way she had run the lead-up to the project submission, taking each day as it came, respecting her somatic self-knowledge and allowing herself to pause, change pace, take time off and resume according to that felt series of guidelines. The process of attending to her own experiencing and the precise differences in the way she processed apparently similar experiences led her to her own individually prescribed solution.

As I learn how my brain works I'll be able to teach others useful skills

As we learn how experience is structured, we begin to realise that what we have learnt is a set of amazing tools. Not only can they be used to improve our lives in other contexts than the ones which brought us for help, but they can also be shared with others. Structures and their varied applications can be taught. The client, or student, has learnt by doing, and they have also learnt intellectually about the interventions they are making. The learning has been at a number of significant levels: it is a whole-person learning. One manager who attended a course Ian ran on leadership skills was immediately able to utilise a particular pattern to help himself understand, feel and act differently in a conflict situation at work. He found this pattern very enabling. Not only did it help him: a few weeks later when two of his employees were also in conflict, he took time to teach each of them the pattern so that they would have skills for resolving their conflict themselves rather than merely relying on him to 'sort it out' for them.

The strategic patterns which NLP originally extrapolated from the work of its first subjects are not simply the property of the therapist: they become part of the client's portfolio, and thus potentially reach out through their lives to those with whom they are in contact. Children can be taught skills that help with their school or college work, the management of their friendships and love affairs, and the alleviation of their own anxieties and stresses. Colleagues, friends and employees may all benefit. Sometimes a skill may be taught formally; but it is more likely that because of the naturalistic way in which the therapy will have worked, the client too will be able to make their interventions and offer their skills naturalistically and informally. The process continues . . .

The greater the clarity the less the judgement

When we become curious about something, we begin to suspend judgement about it. This is extremely important in the effects it has on the way we approach both ourselves and others. Clients who have for a long time despised themselves for their behaviour or feelings, once they become curious about how this process happens and how the process is often reliably maintained despite evidence to the contrary, begin to see how it makes sense. A client who said that as far as she was concerned everything she did was 'crap', and that if someone (even someone she loved and trusted) paid her a compliment she would automatically think they were mistaken, or having her on, was invited to speculate on what putting herself down in this way might achieve for her. Like most people encountering the notion of positive intent for the first time, she needed time to consider the very idea; but once it had been repeated and clarified she immediately said 'because it stops other people knocking me down'. The rapidity and clarity of her own answer somewhat surprised her, and it was clear from her thoughtful demeanour and more active involvement in the rest of the session that this alone had been a liberating intervention.

A manager who was under great pressure was castigating himself for failing to prioritise sufficiently. When asked what would happen if he did prioritise better, he immediately said this would mean using his diary more to allocate time, that this in turn would involve saying 'no' to many people who wanted him to do this and that, and that this would involve him on many fronts in conflict and confrontation, which he hated and would find difficult. Once he understood that his 'poor' prioritising actually had an unconscious protective function, he blamed himself less – and was able to seek support for saying no and dealing with the expected consequences.

Curiosity that is stimulated by the recognition that behaviour – even self- or other- destructive behaviour – has both a positive intent and a purposeful structure becomes self-perpetuating and generalising: if this behaviour had a purpose, the implication is that other behaviours do too. If this had a clear shape and sequence, patterns are likely to underlie other internal experiences. Generalisation is one of the main ways in which we both simplify the mass of data available to us and seek to predict the future on the basis of past learning: we can often see how this process can be limiting (as for example in the increasingly inclusive scope of phobic reactions), but how much more liberating and exciting, for both client and therapist, to recognise that life-enhancing strategies and interpretations can also extend their scope to encompass wider and wider areas of our lives.

I can get much more out of this than I thought I could

Clients frequently come to therapy with a specific goal, which as we said at the outset of this book is often quite limited. Because of the way in which the brain generalises, the client's learnings in the therapeutic context will frequently be discovered to have a much wider application. We can say that the changes are generative. For example, a young man whose childhood as the son of a wealthy but alcoholic and violent father and passive mother had left him closed off and lacking in social confidence, began to learn to value himself more and to establish a healthier distance from his family's repeated manipulation. As a result, he completed the part-time degree he had started, was offered a place on an MBA, and when internal politics at work threatened to draw him in went directly to the Managing Director saying that he was not prepared to be caught up and made a pawn in others' machinations, and offered his resignation. As a result of this bold move it became clear that his MD was anxious to retain him: he was offered a salary increase and, if he wanted it, guaranteed employment at the same level in his native Australia. Asked to say how much he wanted, he asked for, and was given, a rise of 50 per cent.

I've learnt to dream a bigger dream

As people begin to realise that problematic feelings or behaviours which they had felt stuck with for years can in fact be changed; as they begin to experience being able to make those changes; as they begin to experience that it is *they* who are making the changes, even though the therapist will be acting as coach and support, the wonderful possibility begins to open up that life could perhaps be more than just like it was before, minus the problem. Perhaps things might change direction altogether. Perhaps they might become the self they have always felt inside that they could be. One client, mentioned earlier, who had been helped to rebuild her confidence and find ways to be less easily dominated by her mother, later reported that in a matter of months she had gone on to take a course in assertiveness and another for adult returners to academic study. She had also experimented with a different, freer style of art work than the tightly controlled illustration by which she had previously made a living, had begun collaborating with a friend made on the assertiveness course to produce a children's book, and had made contact again with her estranged brother.

It will be clear from the examples in this chapter that many people who initially come for help in an NLP context find that they get more than they expected. They may initially hope that their problem will be ameliorated with the help of an expert; but they are likely to discover that they themselves possess far more resources than they had first supposed, that their difficulties can often be considered as the result not of intrinsic faults or failures but rather of appropriate but limited learning, and that their developing skills in managing their own processing can serve them flexibly in many contexts beyond those of the 'presenting problem'.

Many, if not most, clients come for therapy in the belief that it will ameliorate their difficulties. While it is our experience that NLP does help people do this very effectively, we usually find that its effects go far beyond the managing of crises and the solving of problems. Because NLP is an active and client-driven way of working, clients learn new skills and new resources; but they also learn to recognise resources they already have and to apply them in new contexts. Through these experiences, many not only acquire a new confidence in themselves but a real curiosity about just what is possible, and an excitement in finding out.

Client benefits Skill-builders

Therapist
- Make it your task with a number of clients to take something they want to change/dislike about themselves and get the client to identify when and in what context this unwanted behaviour would be a useful skill/attribute. You will need to presuppose in your use of language that this can in fact be useful ('when' and 'how' are both good presupposing lead-ins here).

Supervisor
- Together with your supervisee, identify a negatively valued client behaviour/attribute and brainstorm its possible usefulness and the contexts in which it might be useful. It's often important here to model true brain-storming. Coming up with a few wild examples helps the individual 'jump out of the box' and become more flexible in their thinking.

7

NLP Benefits to the Therapist

It is because I find value and reward in human relationships that I
enter into a relationship known as therapeutic, where feelings and
cognition merge into one unitary experience which is lived rather
than examined, in which awareness is non-reflective, and where I
am participant rather than observer. But because I am curious
about the exquisite orderliness which appears to exist in the
universe and in this relationship I can abstract myself from the
experience and look upon it as an observer, making myself and/or
others the objects of that observation. As observer I use all of the
hunches which grow out of the living experience.

(Carl Rogers, *On Becoming a Person*, 1967: 223)

It may seem unusual in a book outlining a particular form of therapy to
look explicitly at what practising in such a way does for the therapist, to
ask the question: 'What's in it for us?' But just as NLP offers the client
experiences and learnings that transform their experience, so it also has
profoundly transforming effects on the therapist. We believe it is not
only legitimate but essential to look at these.

If the core work of the therapeutic encounter is understood to be
helping the client ameliorate painful, traumatic, limiting, distorting
experiences, it appears to follow at some emotional level that this will
probably be a less than delightful experience for the therapist. But why?

What if the task is reframed as one of sharing with the client in a
process of learning, self-transformation, enlargement of resources and
skills − by means of which their experience can be restructured with
ease and effectiveness, so that their lives can become fuller, more
enriching, more exciting, beyond their original limited hopes? An exciting
process to share in, indeed. And what if, in order to do this, the therapist
has similar experiences, not just in training but in day-to-day living?
There is then the possibility of an encounter which is shared at a core
level of meaning. The experience of the client parallels that of the
therapist; the experience of the therapist parallels that of the client. The
process is one of engagement in the discovery, enjoyment and utilisation
of the possibilities that come with one's own unique humanity. Over and
above these task-related benefits, we have noticed that working with
NLP offers its practitioners benefit on another dimension: that of
personal energy and vibrancy. Clients find it energising to experience
− perhaps for the first time − a sense of personal resourcefulness; to

learn immediately usable skills; to understand how they presently structure their experience and how to retain what works for them and
modify what limits them. This is an exciting process – and it is exciting to
work with.

Since its collaborative beginnings, NLP has sought to understand, to
explicate and to pass on, the structure of excellence. Its roots, its
development and its values are inclusive. We believe that this means it
has much to offer counsellors and therapists from many different
backgrounds, working in many different settings.

If you can discover a truly excellent way to do something, you can
codify and teach it: others can learn it. In identifying over the years so
many of the ways in which subjective experience is structured, and so
many of the implications this has for improving communication, NLP has
provided us with recipes which can be relied upon, and which in turn can
be creatively varied, referred to and taken yet further.

Since NLP is inclusive, it does not automatically rule out certain
moods or approaches as being unsuitable for therapy: humour can have a
place, as can playfulness. Stimulating discussions can be part of it. It is
varied, from client to client, from session to session, from moment to
moment – according to what is needed and appropriate. Varied fare for
both parties. Both the therapist and client become more versatile, more
flexible, more personally resourceful, as a result.

This chapter, therefore, takes as its base not merely the right of the
therapist to find benefits in the work in which they are engaged, but the
necessity and inevitability of their doing so. It explores some of the
personal as well as professional benefits. Let's look at these individually.
For the sake of clarity, we have grouped them under a number of
headings; but of course the experience itself is seamless. We have
personalised the headings as a way of reflecting our experience.

Benefits at the level of skill

*We gain new tools, techniques and interventions and above
all new ways of thinking*
In sharing their observations of the structure of *what worked*, the
various developers of NLP have provided therapists with a number
of highly effective procedures for helping clients to make the changes
they desire. In practice, effective therapists work their own variations
upon the procedures they have learnt, much as great cooks have their
own versions of the major recipes; but the underlying principle
guides the work and leads to its successful conclusion. Processes such
as reimprinting and the fast phobia cure have helped numerous
clients, and will continue to help many more, because they work.

These procedures are the more obvious face of NLP. More important, in our view, are some of its underlying attitudes and assumptions, some of which have been explored in detail in the chapter on presuppositions and others which appear in a fuller list at the end of the book. If we had to summarise the most central of these, we would say inclusiveness, reflexiveness, respect, curiosity and modelling, all of which have threaded their way through our story so far. This means that we can use NLP in conjunction with many therapeutic approaches and in varied professional contexts.

Our sensory acuity is enhanced
Working with NLP both requires that we pay careful attention to sensory information of all kinds, and teaches us how to develop and refine our ability to do so. The more we notice the full range of information that is available to us, the more well-grounded are our hypotheses, the more rapid our ability to assess the changing state of the client and to relate it to what is going on – whether or not we know consciously what that is, and whether or not the client knows it consciously either. This means that we acquire a sophisticated monitoring system, which can also be taught to the client as part of their self-development. Where we notice, we can reflect; where they notice, they can tune in more effectively to their own responses and to those of others. Like all skills, the skill of sensory acuity may first be enhanced through deliberate effort, becoming more automatic and elegant as it becomes more habitual. But like all skills, it consists of learnable how-to's which NLP can deliver. With such sensitive antennae to unconsciously generated information, the therapist has a source of information which complements what is said or done at a conscious level, and which frequently helps to open up a richer world of internal meaning that informs the work of the therapy. For example, a therapist may notice that although the client is saying something positive, there is an argument psychologically: the 'yes' needs to be checked in case there is a 'no' at some other level. Skin colour, muscle tone and expression may change. Perhaps the client gradually, or sometimes suddenly, looks younger, and the therapist may begin to wonder if a childhood experience or feeling has been triggered. Often these changes are small and subtle; but we do not need to wait for years of therapeutic experience to enhance our ability to notice and act on them.

We become more flexible

FLEXIBLE THINKING   Where fundamental structures are understood, it becomes easier to work out what is going on, and to select appropriate interventions. We showed earlier, for example, how an understanding of the logical levels can help us understand the relationship between where a problem is experienced, where it originates and where it can most easily be changed. Such a tool offers us both information and a guide to effective intervention. Most importantly, it offers us a number of possibilities rather than just one. We may work with it explicitly or implicitly; we may work at the level of the experience or the origin. We may help the client reframe their felt experience of the problem by addressing it on a different level. For example, by drawing attention to how a problem behaviour may be acting as a defence for, or an expression of, identity, we may enable the client to acknowledge its purposefulness, and to seek more acceptable or less inconvenient means of achieving the same end. Conversely, by helping them recognise that what has always been treated within their family as an issue of identity can more properly be seen as an issue of behaviour, we may help them realise that a label (for example, 'lazy', or 'difficult') does not have to be taken as an integral part of the self but can be accepted – if at all – as relating to a chosen response to certain circumstances . . . and can therefore become one of many possible options, rather than the only, or characteristic, one.

For example, the manager whose organisation was being pressured by its backers to make changes more rapidly than it could implement and its staff accommodate, began to wonder whether he lacked the necessary skills for the job. His counsellor began to consider the problem in the context of logical levels: was it one of the manager's *capability*? Was it due to a clash of *beliefs* between the backers and the staff? Or, since the backers were concerned that the organisation was overtrading, was it perhaps one of *behaviour*? Considering the problem in this way gave the counsellor a variety of options – the first of which was to share these possibilities with the client, so that together they could select an appropriate level for intervention.

FLEXIBLE BEHAVIOUR   A principle identified early on in the development of NLP was that of 'requisite variety': in any situation the person with the greatest flexibility is the one with the greatest potential influence. A therapist's capacity to influence his or her clients therapeutically therefore relates directly to their own range of available responses and skills. For example, if through no fault of their own a client is late for an appointment both they and the therapist could assume that there was insufficient time left for a 'proper' session – or, the therapist might ask 'Given the time we have today, what's the most useful thing we can do together?' The presupposition is that there might be many useful things they could do – and that the client will know which is the one that might be of greatest help. This underscores the client's ownership of the therapy while at the same time directing them to the best therapeutic option.

Another example might occur during an established pattern of therapy, where client and therapist might be expecting a particular pattern of interaction or focus based on their experience of working together so far. However, some event in the client's life disrupts their expectations and the state which they have come to associate with therapy. They arrive angry because they have tried for 20 minutes to find a parking space; they are tense because of an unexpected and unwelcome visit by an in-law; they have had a sleepless night because of a teething baby. With its emphasis on pacing, NLP helps both therapist and client to work from what is, not what ought to be, and to find ways in which addressing the client's immediate situation can become of wider use to the client, often generating further understanding and growth.

We find it easy to map across from different situations, different metaphors, different approaches

Where a structure is understood, similar ones can be recognised, in whatever context they occur. This opens up to us a wealth of possibilities: experience can be enriched through the use of complementary metaphors, we can identify how effective structures in other areas of a client's experience may be borrowed to enrich or transform situations in which they are currently experiencing difficulties, or to replicate their own structures of excellence where they are most needed. We can use our understanding to identify precisely where problematic structures differ from ones which initially appear similar but which have enabling outcomes, and to target needed changes. We can help clients – and ourselves – build upon what they and we do well, and to generalise from it in life-enhancing ways. A familiarity with underlying patterns brings a dexterity in handling, even playing with them – which can be passed on to the client to enrich their experience and also extend their skills.

For example, a client who had been bullied as a child and who was often, as an adult, still frightened of her mother, started to learn how to be more assertive. In talking about one such episode, she said how she had told her mother to 'back off' from criticising her. Knowing that she bred and trained dogs, her therapist helped her to realise how her own words precisely indicated the approach that was needed in 'retraining' her mother to a better sense of boundaries: firmness and clarity without anger were likely to be the most effective approach – as they had been in this instance.

We improve our ability to manage state changes
Through its recognition of the way in which experience is individually and characteristically constructed, NLP has helped to open up an understanding of how we can recognise and manage our mind–body 'states'. For each of us, what we may think of, and label as, emotions (fear, panic, excitement, anxiety) have their physiological and mental correlates. As the section on mind–body experience showed, complex psycho-physiological patterning makes up much experience in a way which often feels overwhelming and beyond the reach of our own intervention. The concept of states offers us a way in, not only to understanding these processes, but to working effectively with them, both in ourselves and others. Once we can describe the characteristics of a state as it is personally constructed, we can identify what are the significant components or triggers: thence, we can begin to discover how simply, readily and swiftly states can be managed and changed. Because even the most deeply felt state is constructed of a number of elements, it follows that a change in one element can change the totality. Innumerable possibilities are opened up. Unwelcome or limiting states can be deconstructed by introducing new, contrasting or incongruous elements; by working within the characteristic representational system or by challenging it.

Because there are so many possibilities, the scope for therapeutic creativity is immense. For the client, the significant learning is that once you know you can change your state, you can never be sure of feeling so helpless again.

The same is true for the practitioner. For all of us, there are times when we are tired, anxious, mildly unwell or lacking focus. If we know what characterises, and can be used to trigger, our own effective 'enabling state', we can ensure that we are best prepared for helping our clients. For example, one counsellor suffered a sudden family bereavement during a weekend. She asked herself whether it was possible, or appropriate, to see the clients who had sessions booked during the following week. None were addressing a similar problem, and she was able to use her own knowledge of state management to ensure that she was in a 'fit state' both to continue to work, and to do her own mourning outside of office hours.

We are able to work with mind–body issues in a new way
Understanding more of how mind and body interconnect at a systemic level opens up a range of fascinating possibilities in therapeutic work. We become aware that useful interventions will have effects throughout; we learn that a whole range of subtle unconscious information is available to us through the client's responses, which can give us reliable information about the efficacy of our work; and we

gain access to physiological processes through their related mental structuring. As we work more at the interface between what used to be thought of as mind and body, we can begin to discover how much is possible in terms of healing, and how it is no longer safe to say confidently 'that can't be done'.

For example, a man in his 60s came for help in losing weight. In discussing with him not just his eating and exercise patterns but his wider experience of life, his therapist discovered that though his long-term marriage had been unhappy for years, he was unable, as a believing Catholic, to leave it. His wife was seriously but chronically unwell, and he was literally 'weighting' for her to die. Meanwhile, he was putting a barrier around his undiminished sexuality so that neither he nor possible partners would be tempted. Working with the metaphor of weight/wait at various levels, and using a number of NLP techniques to assist the client in addressing his situation more directly, the therapist helped the client to lose more than six inches round his waist, and four inches in collar size, so that he was able to achieve a greater harmony with his physical self without violating his value-system.

We are able to establish clear evidence procedures for change
NLP affords us a number of important ways to check on whether desired change is occurring. Enhanced sensory acuity allows us, as we have said, to become more aware of subtle, physiological responses in the client, which provide an ongoing way of monitoring what is happening for them at unconscious as well as conscious levels. Specific procedures make use of this in more structured ways, allowing us to check whether change has been, or will be made, and also to establish before the change is carried out in practice that its impact throughout the client's entire system is acceptable (a procedure known in NLP as 'the ecology check'). When the client is asked at the beginning of therapy what it is that they want, they will be assisted to formulate and refine their goals according to a set of conditions which NLP has developed to ensure, in advance, that desired outcomes are well formed for success. Part of this procedure involves asking how they will know if it is being achieved – a question which elicits specific changes that will result at behavioural and feeling levels. These then give therapist and client a series of criteria by which the degree of the change can be measured. Formulating a realistic and achievable goal at the outset means there is no need for either client or therapist to fudge the issue later: we are not going to be saying 'well, we didn't get the change, but we did get something else, so that's nice'. There is a real rigour in the procedure which is helpful to both parties. Where the desired change doesn't result, or is less in

extent than was expected, they know that something else needs addressing: perhaps this therapist has reached the limits of their skill; perhaps there is some other factor, previously unrecognised, inhibiting change. Both of these are genuine issues, which can be honoured and openly discussed.

For example, an elderly lady came for help with chronic IBS. She was in almost constant pain, and had to spend up to six hours a day, in short bursts, in the lavatory. She had been living with her husband, who had suffered a foot amputation during the Korean war, and a disabled daughter. Their house was large and unmodernised, and the client needed to 'run up and down' a great deal. While therapy was able to ameliorate her IBS, and to shift the pain around so that it was not always in one place, it did not remove it. Open discussion led them to the conclusion that the client needed a genuine reason to have some time to herself and to enjoy privacy to escape from drudgery – which she did by reading romances in the toilet. Without her IBS she would have felt obliged to do even more for her disabled husband and daughter. It was important that genuine pain and a degree of disability remained, as it was not within this client's belief-system to challenge the long-term patterns of her family role-relationships. She was grateful for the improvement she obtained, knew she could achieve more when she chose, and the therapist was able to feel satisfied with the degree of success, rather than feeling she had failed.

We have more choices, so that we can experience being more resourceful with more clients
Once we understand the basic structures which underlie subjective experience, and how to elicit from individual clients the specific ways in which they structure theirs, it becomes possible to work with ever greater refinement with them, matching not simply our interventions but our whole way of communicating more effortlessly with the client's characteristic processing. As we have also shown, paying this kind of attention to clients at a number of levels allows us to pick up the often very precise information they unconsciously give about what kinds of things need to happen for their desired changes to take place. This increases both the range and accuracy of our resource-fulness. It also means that the limitations we may have previously recognised in our clinical work – 'I'm less happy working with children', 'I find it difficult to sympathise with manipulative/obsessive clients', for example – may begin to disappear. 'Sympathy' literally means 'feeling with': once we have learnt *how* this client constructs their experience of the world, it becomes much easier to get alongside them; the curiosity about how they do that which is so characteristic of NLP can create a very different frame of mind.

Benefits at the level of ideology and theoretical understanding

We gain an understanding of some of the most fundamental coding mechanisms of the brain

This is because, as we have shown, NLP is not based on a hypothesis about how and why people function as they do, but on useful maps that enable us to offer practical interventions. We could see this as being like the scientific attempts to describe a newly discovered terrain: more information is always being added; new patterns that facilitate change are being developed; but what we have is as exact a description, in universally understandable and usable terms, as explorers and map-makers can at any one time provide. While NLP recognises that the map is not the territory, it is also as reliable a guide for getting about in the landscape as we have. This works both at the meta level of understanding, as with the logical levels, and at a more specific level of structuring, such as that of the preferred representational system coding of an individual client's experience. Rather like maps, these constructs provide us with ways of representing different features of the territory, which guide our explorations.

For example, a finals student who had been seeking help for anxiety phoned in a panic after one of his papers. His NLP counsellor asked what kind of a panic it was, and he described how he kept going over the information he had missed out, and how he would therefore fail the paper. This was having such a debilitating effect that he feared he wouldn't be able to attend his examination the following day. His counsellor asked him *how* he kept going over what he had missed, and it became clear that he was *telling himself* – in other words, that his panic was operating largely through internal dialogue. The counsellor asked him to repeat the process briefly, and (since their conversation was on the telephone) asked in what direction his eyes were looking as he listened to himself in this way. The student said he was looking down and to the left, which suggested to the counsellor that an intervention which shifted his eye-focusing might help scramble the debilitating pattern. Accordingly, she asked the student to remember something very encouraging that he had heard from someone he trusted: he quickly found an example of being told by one of his tutors how able he was. The counsellor asked him to look down left again and let the pattern begin again – but as soon as it did, to look horizontally left instead and hear his tutor's encouraging words. As he did this, the student began to feel calmer and more confident again. Once the counsellor had discovered exactly how the student was constructing his anxiety, she was able to use his patterning to help him transform the situation and take himself into a more resourceful state. Both the panic and the calm confidence were features of the student's private territory; neither was in any absolute sense 'truer' than the other; but in terms of his immediate situation one was definitely a better and more productive place to be.

We gain a meta-description of different ways of working
which will underpin our understanding of what is successful
Since NLP offers us ways of describing both underlying structures and their individual components, it gives us as clinicians a way of describing our own interventions. The inspired, intuitive intervention which was really transforming may, at the time, be as much the result of rapid, effective unconscious processing as ever; but when we examine it afterwards we have the means to recognise why and how it worked. We can then benefit as learners from our own successful experience, and be able to replicate it, enhancing in the process our confidence as well as our skill. Moreover, we come to understand on a much wider front how it is that many different approaches all 'work'. As returning to the roots of NLP reminds us, good clinical practice and good communication have a common structure, which will be operating whatever the theoretical underpinning and whatever the nature of the chosen interventions. This allows us, in turn, to retain a respect for what is distinctive in the way we – and our chosen discipline – go about things, while enhancing our respect for different kinds of effective practitioners coming from different traditions. There is room for all of us.

A therapist had seen a young woman on a number of occasions. Among other concerns, the client was trying to decide whether to break off her current relationship and go back to a former boyfriend, who had offered her more excitement but less stability than her current partner. When she came for another session, client and therapist found themselves discussing the difficulty of clearing 'clutter'. The client had previously mentioned that she saved items that might one day be useful, and had lamented her inability to sort out her overcrowded living room. Although the therapist was initially puzzled about the direction the session was taking, she had learnt from experience that overt concerns were often related to underlying needs, and was prepared to trust that she could accept what the client was offering as in some way symbolic of the issues that confronted her. Because the apparently casual conversation – prompted by an article both had read in the paper – seemed in some way charged, the therapist continued to explore with the client the positive values of keeping options open by not throwing things away, the length of time it might take to realise that they were not in fact going to be wanted, and how she felt about useful versus decorative objects. Resolving the issue at the level at which it was offered helped towards a resolution at a deeper level. If we use the logical levels model, this might be because of a correspondence between external behaviour and the person's values or even identity. If we examine the process from another angle, it might be that the client was coding emotional clutter in the same way (using the same representational system sequencing) as physical clutter. In the event, after a light-hearted and quite stimulating discussion, the client concluded that she could apply what she had learnt about managing physical clutter to help her make needed decisions about her relationships. Later in supervision the therapist said 'now I understand the power of metaphor'.

We learn to know from experience that fast and lasting change has a structure and are reminded of how easy it can be
We have already discussed the 'fast is phoney' myth earlier in the book; but it is well ingrained in the culture at large. Every successful, fast experience we have as clinicians, that we are able to predict and bring about as a result of our understanding of how experience is structured and changed, helps us become confident that fast change can be easy and lasting. This in turn builds into a cycle of increasing confidence for ourselves and our clients. Many NLP procedures help us and our clients in this way. Using them to recode past traumas or limiting decisions, which can happen very rapidly, can give us confidence in the real possibilities of fast and lasting change. Reframing, for example, is one way in which significant changes can happen almost instantaneously. Rather like the moment of apprehending that the drawing of the two faces can also be seen as a vase, a reframe adds another possibility to the way we can interpret a situation. Once you have that possibility, you can choose not to use it – but you can't choose not to have it. The way you structure the original information has been fundamentally altered. Thus, even a conversational reframe can have profound effects on the way a client structures a problem or difficulty, a limiting belief or past learning.

Benefits at the level of practice

We are able to work much faster with certain issues
Because NLP has been able to identify and describe the structure of some processes which people have in common, for example, phobias or repetitive unwanted behaviours, therapists working with NLP

have access to a number of proven strategies which ensure effective work. It becomes possible to distinguish between the underlying structure and the way it is individually patterned by the client, so that the patterning is matched in order to bring about a successful, individually tailored change-process.

One student on an NLP training course, for example, had only just learnt the fast phobia cure when his teenage daughter came home from a party one night, slipped on the wet basement steps and injured herself badly on a broken milk-bottle. She had been phobic about hospitals from an incident in childhood, and became very agitated when she realised that she would have to go to outpatients for immediate treatment. As they waited for the ambulance, her father took her through the steps of the fast phobia cure, and was able in those relatively few minutes to help her so transform her experience that the hospital held no dread for her. As a result, she was calm while the glass was removed and the wounds cleaned and stitched, commenting that she just knew she would now never need to fear hospitals again.

We trigger less resistance
Resistance is sometimes important information, as we have discussed earlier; but no therapist wants to trigger it accidentally or unnecessarily. Working with NLP gives us invaluable ways of communicating with the client within their own framework – 'talking to them in their own language' – in a highly specific and enriched way. The working relationship thus becomes easier, more congruent, and even challenging interventions can be received by the client without a loading of judgement or a sense that the therapist has a discordantly different perspective on the world. For example, a client who had been sexually abused in childhood, developed in her adult relationships a complex pattern of depending on men, while at the same time pushing them emotionally until they showed a strong reaction – at which point she was able to 'tell them what for'. The therapist built a strong rapport with this client at a number of levels, pacing the hurt adult and wounded child as they variously presented themselves in the working sessions. Eventually, he was able to ask the client how it felt to be able to tell a man what she really thought of his behaviour, thus enabling the client herself to recognise the satisfaction she eventually derived at the end of the repeating series of interactions. Such an intervention could have been very challenging to the client; but because she herself identified the behaviour, its causes and its consequences as a result of her therapist's curious prompting – which in turn prompted her own curiosity – any possible resistance, together with the issue of relative blame, was avoided.

We think on our feet more effectively
NLP, as we have shown, helps us become more attentive to information across the whole sensory and linguistic range, and it also gives us an understanding of what Bandler and Grinder (1975), following the works of Naom Chomsky, recognised as the 'deep structure' of the mind's experiencing. Thus cued in, the therapist is able to make quicker and more apposite interventions: the information is readily available, the client's own 'prescriptions' are recognised in their embedded form, rapport and matching all enable major changes to be made 'by the way' in the course of natural conversation as well as through the more obvious and structured procedures.

A counsellor helping a teenager heard on a number of occasions how much the client 'hated English' at school. One explanation was that this was a reaction to the sudden death of the client's previous English teacher in a car-crash, and her dislike of the less supportive staff-member who took over in her place. Initially responding within this framework, the counsellor suddenly 'heard' the client say that she 'found Italian really difficult'. The client's parents were Italian, and the client had lived in both countries at different times in response to the demands of her father's job. As the counsellor found these two pieces of information coming together, he asked: 'Do you find being Italian and English difficult to manage?', to which the client said a heartfelt 'yes'. Hating 'English' and finding 'Italian' really difficult had more than one meaning: the problem was being experienced at the level of schoolwork (capability) but was picking up a substantial extra charge from issues of identity.

We can walk our talk more effectively
We have throughout emphasised the inclusiveness of NLP in two senses: firstly, that it is based on the universals of human sensory structuring and effective human communication; secondly, that because of this, the therapist enhances their knowledge, skills and range of available options just as the client does. This example of parallel process ensures a congruence between the two therapeutic partners: what the client discovers and learns, the therapist has also discovered and learnt. There is no inbuilt superiority, only a longer history.

Because of this enhanced congruence, we naturally become more influential
Where congruence of this kind is perceived, it carries great conviction, and greater influence. As practitioners, we are sharing knowledge and skills whose efficacy we have already discovered, and are continually re-experiencing. Whether or not therapists choose to

offer information from their own personal experience, it will inform their conviction and enhance their credibility.

We'll almost certainly get a reputation for being very
effective – our practices will flourish
Genuineness, congruence and unconditional positive regard: Carl Rogers' recipe for an effective therapist. Where these are experienced in a setting which also offers effective, fast, accessible, learnable and non-distressing interventions, clients will be helped in a way which deals swiftly and effectively with their presenting issues, gives them the experience of owning not only the problem but the resources for its solution, and avoids retraumatising. In addition, the skills they learn in relation to their presenting problem will have relevance and applications far beyond, becoming truly generative of further learning, further mastery. They are very likely to spread the word! Many NLP therapists get phone messages that begin: 'You don't know me but you helped a friend of mine.'

We become more aware of our own epistemology and get to
know the presuppositions we are employing and that
underpin our working
We have arrived where we are today as therapists as a result of the unique interaction of our personal characters, histories and training. The beliefs that underpin the clinical work we do are drawn from all these roots, some explicitly, some implicitly and unconsciously. Even where training has involved personal therapy or analysis, the emphasis of that personal experience may have addressed issues likely to be problematic for ourselves or our clients rather than helping us to explore the resourcefulness of our life-learning, or to consider the interconnected implications of our assumptions and beliefs at the different logical levels of our existence. Yet these things are of great importance in both our personal and our professional lives. In learning how to work with NLP, we cannot but learn more about ourselves, about how to restructure encodings which may be less helpful and how to make even fuller use of resources which are enabling for ourselves and those whom we are seeking to help.

We gain a much clearer understanding of the structure of
what we do well and so become able to replicate our own best
practice reliably
Many therapists' most inspired interventions are intuitive, particularly as we become sufficiently experienced to have reached the level of unconscious competence. Nonetheless, an understanding of the structures of communication allows us to answer the sometimes

frustrating question 'Now how did I do that?' when we couple it with attentive recall and client feedback. The feedback, of course, does not need to be verbal: as we replay in our minds how a particularly effective session went, the heightened sensory acuity which we will have developed through NLP affords us markers for significant interventions in terms of how the client responded: a state change at *this* point, a volunteering of new information in response to *that*, an illuminating re-connection just *then*. The ability to replay is itself improved, since so much more information can be noted and stored across a greater range of sensory modalities.

Self-care and self-development

So far in this chapter, we have talked a good deal about how NLP enhances our skills as clinical practitioners. But what about what it does for us as people-who-happen-to-be-therapists? Therapists work in many settings, where client numbers, severity of problems, multiple or divided accountability, limited resources and administrative support can constrain their ability to work at their fullest, most expressive and creative capacity. Even in private practice, the need to earn a living and, perhaps as significantly for many, the sense of day-to-day aloneness cause stress. It is from such pressures as these that many therapists begin to lose the joyfulness in what they are doing, to feel increasingly eroded and eventually burnt out.

In our experience, NLP is a very renewing therapeutic modality to work in. As an ongoing means of self-exploration, learning and development, it brings us continual stimulus. The more we know about how people operate – not as groupings, classifications or generalities but as very unique constructors of very unique worlds of experience – the more likely it is that each session will entice us with *new curiosity* and different processes. Further, it offers us a wealth of means of managing our own stress, allowing us to manage that tenuous and enticing borderline between empathic involvement and necessary distancing with skill and appropriateness for both parties. It offers us, in other words, *a very powerful anti-burnout measure*.

In common with other developing skills, it offers us the possibility of increased *playfulness* – a delight not only in our own abilities, but in those of our clients as they first tentatively, then confidently, try out some of the creative possibilities NLP offers. Because it emphasises *what works*, there is space within it for jokes, for word-play, for anecdote, for experimentation. There are no intrinsic hard-and-fast rules about the 'right' kind of process or tone.

Because working with these tools involves using them to work on ourselves, we *become clearer about our own needs* as well. As we have shown, the increased attentiveness and curiosity which is character-istic of NLP cannot just be applied to the client: it is an awareness which, once learnt, is life-transforming. Of course, we have choices about whether and when we are more or less reflective: NLP brings us more choices rather than taking choices away. But what is once learnt is permanently available to us, and increases our ability to respond to and take care of our own needs, both on- and off-duty. If we are accustomed to paying attention to our clients across a full range of information, it becomes automatic that we do the same for ourselves.

One therapist we knew had eczema, and noticed that it became worse when he was overworking. Accordingly, he 'did a deal' with his other-than-conscious mind: if he was working within his health-and-safety limits, the eczema would disappear; but if he overworked it was to reappear in his elbow crease, where its message would be obvious to him without being discernible by others, and he promised himself that he would then as soon as possible limit the number of his appointments or arrange a holiday. By this means he turned a symptom into a very useful feedback mechanism.

In addressing our own limiting beliefs we become more congruent

Because the tools of NLP are learnt by doing, they are 'in the muscle' rather than simply 'in the head' (or just 'in the books'). We have available to us a rich working repertoire of skills that help us address our own issues, our own blocks and limiting beliefs, in an ongoing process of learning and self-transformation. This makes us more congruent as therapists in two ways: firstly, the message conveyed to the client both implicitly and explicitly is that we 'walk our talk': we are not asking them to do anything we have not ourselves success-fully experienced. For example, if we are helping clients to decrease their stress levels by taking time for themselves, our work is much more congruent if we already do this for ourselves – whether or not that information is shared explicitly with the client. Secondly, our increasing personal congruence places our professional work on a firmer footing, where our own sense of internal ease and harmony makes us less likely to skew or distort our perceptions of what is going on for the client, and gives us greater energy and attentiveness to place at their service.

The benefits of taking a training

We can learn a great deal from books – and indeed it is our hope that you will find this one helps you discover many things which are relevant to your learning and professional practice. However, we also believe that some things are best learnt in a shared and supported context (much as therapy differs from reading self-help books). So we would like to take a little time to outline what, in our experience, you would have to gain by learning in a structured, shared and supported context.

If you take a practitioner training, you will learn by doing,
which gets the knowledge 'into the muscle'
We hope that in in the process of reading this book you will have become intrigued by NLP at a number of levels, and that you will have discovered enough about how it works, on the one hand, and how it feels, on the other, to become curious about learning. The suggestions offered at intervals throughout the book offer you one way to sample some NLP ways of working on an immediate basis, finding out first-hand how it can enrich your own personal repertoire. Nonetheless, there is a limit to how much we can learn from books.

There is a proverb in Papua-New Guinea: 'Until it's in the muscle it's only a rumour'. NLP had its roots in workshops, as many of the early, seminal books reflect in their informal, lively transcript format. NLP training nowadays remains true to that learning-through-doing approach: since we structure our internal experience with reference to our rich and varied sensory processing, it makes sense that learning which involves our major sensory systems – seeing, hearing and the kinesthetic – offers us the richest potential opportunity of truly holistic learning. Sharing that process with lively, many-talented people from a range of different professional backgrounds makes being a student on an NLP training an exciting, moving, stimulating and transforming experience. And the learning is there for immediate, natural professional and personal use – because it is 'in the muscle'. The example we gave earlier of the student who was able to give real and lasting help so soon after 'doing' the fast phobia cure on his training course shows how much confidence comes from this way of learning. In that real emergency there was no room for any lack of conviction, nor for any second attempts. He knew it would work because he had already experienced it working.

You will have experience of how the structures work from
three different positions: subject, practitioner, observer
One of the skills which NLP helps people develop is that of shifting position: not merely understanding but internally experiencing events from inside 'the other person's shoes'. This has great value in many interpersonal situations, both domestic and professional, with applications in conflict resolution, teaching and presenting as well as in

helping to improve personal relationships. One way in which this facility is repeatedly exercised and developed in training is through the use of a three-person format: students practise a skill three times, rotating through the roles of subject, practitioner and observer. The experiencing of being both subject and practitioner is common to many courses, where students are paired to learn and experience a skill: the addition of the observer role provides an invaluable opportunity of honing vital sensory acuity and seeing how the skills actually work in practice. We try things out, we are able to test their efficacy immediately; we can experience the differences that new understanding and procedures make; we can see, hear, feel, the results. The additional learning-by-doing is so that we can rotate through these same roles in our heads in any situation in which we find ourselves: we can develop our ability to empathise; we can become more effective in our self-monitoring by watching how we ourselves operate. And so can our clients.

*You'll learn a technology for achieving an internal locus of
control for yourself, which you can teach to clients*
It is difficult to overestimate how empowering it can be to know from experience that we can make the kind of changes in internal structuring that NLP gives us the knowledge and the power to do. The ability to comprehend how our experience is constructed, and to know not only that we can alter it if we need or wish, and how to go about that successfully, is both liberating and exciting. Training gives us both the know-how and the personal experience, and provides us with a secure base from which we can share the learnings and the skills with our clients.

*You will be confident in your understanding of the structure
of magic, and your ability to work with it*
The way our minds work is truly magic – and that magic has a structure. Knowing the structure from the inside, both in the ways it is shared and in the important ways in which it is individualised, gives us a confidence in communicating with others at every level of our lives, in facilitating life-enhancing processes and securing personal and professional best practice. This confidence comes from a secure experiential understanding, enhanced and developed to its fullest through a training which models what it teaches – as in turn we can model what we teach to our clients in our therapy rooms.

Therapist benefits Skill-builders

Therapist
- Improving sensory acuity. Make a point of watching your clients' eye-movements. Notice how they move, and how the movements precede what is verbally articulated. Become curious about any patterns or sequences you observe, either generally or in relation to a particular client.

Supervisor
- Our resourcefulness is a function of our state as well as of our life experience and skill base. How can you as a supervisor:

  - pay attention to the supervisee's state and
  - help them to a more resourceful state which would help them be even more effective as a person and as a therapist?

For example, you might set yourself the task of monitoring facial expression and muscle tone, body posture, pace, pitch, tone and clarity of speech when the supervisee is talking about something they did well or feel confident about, and compare this carefully with the same behavioural features when they are talking about something they are doubtful or anxious about. You might draw their attention to the differences you have observed, and ask them to deliberately adopt those which go along with the confidence experiences while they talk about the doubtful ones. What differences do they, and you, notice? It may help to move back and forth a number of times to help elicit 'the difference that makes a difference'. (This intervention can also be used with clients, of course.)

Part 3
NLP in Action

8

Case Studies

In an indeterminate world man's central task becomes that of
giving form to the act of living itself; it is up to him to imagine new
possibilities for being human, new ways of how to live, and to
attempt to realize them in practice.
(John Shotter, *Images of Man in Psychological Research*, 1975: 111)

Throughout the book we have used case examples to illustrate our
themes, and we have included some brief examples of dialogue to give
you the flavour of the kind of conversations which actually take place
between client and therapist.

We hope that by now we have given you an understanding of the
ways in which NLP therapists and their clients co-create a working
experience of brief therapy in order to help bring about the changes
that the client wants. With its focus on processes and outcomes, NLP
therapy can be rapid; and we have chosen two typical examples to
present more fully. One is a six-session case, the other a single-session.
NLP techniques can, of course, also be used effectively as part of
longer-term therapeutic work.

The first case, that of Gerry, gives an account of each session with its
issues and therapeutic interventions; and we have added a more analytic
commentary. Ana's case, which follows, is given in dialogue without
commentary.

In both cases we wish that you could see this in video because so
much of what NLP has to offer relates to paying attention to
physiology and how it changes – accessing cues being an obvious case
in point. Nevertheless, we think that you will gain at least some of the
flavour from this very partial and necessarily incomplete linguistic
representation.

Gerry   .

*Gerry was a businessman who attended for six sessions, presenting with
severe headaches and difficulties in sleeping. He explained that he had
first consulted his doctor, who had confirmed that there were no organic
causes, and had then made the referral.*

First session

Background
A fine-drawn, slight man in his late 40s, Gerry appeared tense and stressed, speaking rapidly while sitting upright and unrelaxed. His colour was pale, and there were dark shadows under his eyes. He explained that for the last few months he had been waking early – about 5 am – and either failing to get back to sleep again or eventually dozing off about 6 am and falling into a deep sleep from which it was difficult to wake. As a result, he was spending the mornings trying to wake himself up, and finding as the day progressed that his concentration was failing. This was particularly galling to him because he had recently been promoted to take charge of a department which needed reorganising, and so work demands were incessant and often unpredictable. Staff morale had slipped under a previous head of department who had been unhappy in the post and 'doing time' before finding another job, so it was essential both that Gerry mastered his new responsibilities quickly and imparted confidence to his team. He wanted to get back to his old habit of sleeping well again, so that he could regain his mental alertness and his ability to manage his demanding job to the level of his real ability.

He had been promoted within the company, moving from another team where he had enjoyed working, and where his abilities were recognised and encouraged by a manager who was happy to allow him freedom to innovate within the department's overall goals. The atmosphere had been professional but relaxed. By contrast, the members of his new department seemed to be looking to him for a 'strong lead', as he described it, and the assistant director who had responsibility for overseeing the department, while ostensibly valuing Gerry's skills, seemed to be forever 'looking over my shoulder', pointing out possible pitfalls and problems. In addition, while the department's role was to monitor, research and make recommendations on the implementation of new IT systems within the company at both central and branch level, the espoused values of innovativeness and lateral problem-solving were in practice contradicted and impeded by a very procedural company culture. 'Virtually every idea we have come up with since I transferred to the department has been blocked,' Gerry said. 'I'm beginning to wonder if I'm any good after all. I seem such a misfit – I can't imagine why they promoted me. This assistant manager wasn't part of the selection process, and I get the feeling he'd have opposed my appointment if he had been. I hate to think of myself like this.'

During the months he had been in the new department, Gerry felt his confidence had plummeted. He said he knew he was well able to do the work – that was why he had applied for the post – and he had believed there was much he could contribute. He had always got on well with colleagues in the past, and had expected to be able to establish in the new department something of the team-approach and task-culture that had worked so well in his previous department. He had looked forward to this, and was disappointed when the new team members seemed reluctant to come up with ideas or to risk brainstorming solutions. 'I'm beginning to think the stuffing had been knocked out of them even before I got there,' he said.

He felt angry with himself for 'giving in'. 'I know I've got what it takes – why can't I just get on and make it happen? A year ago, I'd have had no doubts. Even when we hit difficulties, I found a way round them.'

After some months of stress, his situation was worsened by unpredictable headaches – and these were what had propelled him into seeing the doctor. Gerry thought they might be related to his increasing tiredness, or perhaps to his lack of appetite. He said he had always found it hard to keep weight on, and since joining the new department he had lost over a stone. He was either too busy or too stressed to want to eat, but had made himself even if he didn't feel hungry because he knew of old that his metabolism seemed to burn fast and he would become even more weary if he didn't. His girlfriend was doing her best to cook him the kind of things he liked. She was supportive, but had a busy life herself as a flight-attendant, so she was often away.

Even when the doctor reassured him that there was no organic cause ('I had begun to wonder about brain tumours . . .') Gerry was irritated with himself: 'I don't need this right now – I've enough on my plate even if I were on top form.' He had been reluctant to take the time off to see the doctor and to come for therapy. 'I'd never have come if the doctor hadn't told me to. I always thought of myself as a strong person: I should be able to cope without dragging other people in. What's the matter with me? Even now, I've got one niggling away.' Asked to describe the headaches, Gerry said they felt like a steel helmet – 'but one that's about half a size too small: it's pressing in all the time. It's not agony, it's just oppressive. It wears away at me.'

Therapist's interventions and comments

Gerry's initial motivation in asking for help, like that of many clients, was to get *away-from* an intolerable situation: This became clear very early in the session when the therapist asked what Gerry wanted from the therapy: he wanted to get rid of his physiological symptoms and be able to resume his working life with his former energy and vigour. He did not 'feel like himself' any more. He came with a problem frame. As the session progressed and more information was given, it became clear that Gerry had another outcome in mind: as well as feeling like himself again he wanted to be able to regain his confidence in his natural way of working, which his new manager's procedural and problem focused approach had substantially undermined. At the end of the session the therapist clarified this: 'So you want to get back to sleeping well again, and to have a clear head for all you need to do. And it feels like you'd also like to be more confident again: you *know* that you've got the skills, you *know* that they can deliver what's needed, but you don't *feel* that at the moment. Right? So being able to feel that again is actually an important part of your goal.' Gerry's heartfelt agreement that this was the case allowed him to go away from the session with a 'towards' motivation, and with a belief that therapy could help him achieve more than he had at first expected. The session had moved from a problem frame to an outcome frame.

Gerry's problem was presented as one of disturbances at a 'behavioural' level: disruptions in sleeping patterns and unpredictable headaches which struck at any time and at home as well as at work. Yet as he talked, it became clear that he had major concerns at much higher levels: his 'beliefs' about his role in the company and about how his department should best go about its tasks were in conflict with those of the assistant manager who had responsibility over him, and the manager's doubting and nit-picking approach had begun to have a considerable impact upon his sense of self. As a professional, his confidence in his professional skills had become part of his sense of 'identity', and Gerry felt his 'capability' was being undermined. The manager was having a negative impact at the very highest of logical levels. Advice which Gerry had sought from colleagues in the old department simply confirmed their belief in him, but gave him no help in dealing with the new situation. In addition, his new manager had sent him on a series of management courses which, in emphasising a very structured and top-down approach, had only exacerbated the situation. He felt he needed help, but had been overwhelmed by 'the wrong kind', thus adding to his problems the belief that he 'could never be the kind of manager that was wanted' (here capability and identity became fused). 'I'm so up against it all I can't see any way forward at the moment.'

The therapist's approach was to pace Gerry in a range of ways: by matching his rather rapid speech at the outset of the session, by inviting him to explore his difficulties in his own way, at his own rate, rather than by asking for formal case-history information, and by recognising and also making use of the strongly kinesthetic and visual language patterns which came naturally to Gerry. In so doing, the therapist quickly and unobtrusively established rapport.

When Gerry mentioned that he had a low-grade headache now, the therapist invited him to describe it in detail, and, somewhat surprised, Gerry did so, in ways which suggested that the headaches might have a metaphoric relationship to the 'tight fit' or mismatch situation he now seemed to be in at work. Gerry had said that he was 'always getting headaches', to which the therapist, with a smile and a raised eyebrow, replied '*Always*?', thus both drawing Gerry's attention to the generalisation and inviting him to explore the contrast between times when he did and times when he didn't. He had evidently not considered this before, and on reflection said that he supposed the headaches were worse when he had something to do which was urgent, or which in some way 'went against the grain', 'like filling in some paltry set of forms or writing a lengthy proposal for something I'd just have been able to get on and do without anyone's formal permission in the old department'.

The therapist suggested that Gerry might like to think of the headaches as letting him know how the situation was pressing on him – in other words, as 'feedback' which could be useful, rather than as a problem. Asked what happened when he had a headache, Gerry replied that sometimes he would 'just have to go for a walk to clear my head'; often the task in hand would take longer, and he would have to put less urgent things aside instead of attempting to do them as well. The therapist drew Gerry's attention to the fact that such consequences had their positive side: the headaches could be said to help him take a needed break (and fresh air), to feel he had to prioritise rather than attempt to do everything.

This 'reframe' of the problem behaviour as having 'positive intent' really surprised – and convinced – Gerry. 'That's given me a lot to think about,' he said when he left. 'I can't quite see how this is going to turn out yet, but I feel it was a good idea to come.' Given a choice of appointments, he decided to come again the following week.

Second session

Gerry phoned the therapist five minutes before his appointment time, saying that he would be late because he had had a 'stupid accident' with his car which had delayed him setting off. Rushed, irritated and angry, he was in fact 15 minutes late. 'The car's quite driveable, but I know it'll be hundreds of pounds worth of work and masses of inconvenience. Forms to fill in, car off the road, all that. And I feel so stupid – I'm not that kind of driver.'

The first half of the session continued in much the same vein – the week at work had been frustrating: contrasting it with this time last year, when he had been in the other department, he felt work had 'lost its zing'. Despite leaving the previous session feeling hopeful, he had had still had some disturbed nights and a couple of severe headaches.

The therapist paced this mood of rush and irritability with a more rapid tempo of speech, verbal acceptance and physical matching. Gerry's gestures were rapid and jerky: the therapist intermittently made notes, then led Gerry to talking about how his normal driving differed from today, encouraging him to explore the similarities without pointing out their possible metaphoric relationship. 'Well, I'm a good driver: quite measured, keep to the speed limits, but decisive – I like to get the best out of the car and the road. That's what made me so angry this morning. You know, it's rather like work: I can do it all but I'm in such a state I'm beginning to cock it up. Then I feel stupid because it need never have happened.'

Gerry began to calm down, reminding himself that the car was insured and that he could call on the company pool to supply him with another. 'Perhaps I'm not really in a fit state to drive at the moment, anyway: maybe it would be better if I went to that meeting in Birmingham on the train. I could relax more – do some work if I need to, catch up on sleep, even.'

Taking the cue from Gerry, the therapist changed to a more relaxed posture, putting the notebook to one side and beginning to speak more slowly. They explored what Gerry would need to do to 'get the car sorted', and talked about how he would prioritise tasks at work so as to make the most of his energies.

This reminded Gerry that he had felt somewhat more in control of his workload since the previous session. Despite the headaches, there had been several days when he had slept better and felt more able to concentrate. While his initial response to the first headache had been the usual one of irritation at his 'weakness', he had remembered after a while the therapist's suggestion that the headaches could be taken as feedback, and asked himself what this one was telling him. 'It felt like it was just telling me I was under pressure,' he said, 'So I gave myself ten minutes to list the things I'd been reminding myself to do that day, and realised there were three or four I could leave for later – another day, well actually next week. It really helped writing it down – then I didn't have to go on carrying it in my head. After that I took a couple of paracetamols and was able to finish the really important things. I made sure I left dead on time, too, so that I could have a shower and a cup of tea in my own good time before my girlfriend was due in.'

By pacing the client's initial state, and by engaging him in plans for sorting the car accident out, the therapist was able to re-anchor the client into a more resourceful state, where he could remind himself that his normal behavior was calmer and more in control. This also allowed him, at an unconscious level, to remind himself that he could take control of the 'crash' situation at work. In this more resourceful state, he was again put in touch with better things that had happened between the sessions, which demonstrated to him and to the therapist that he had been able to use the learnings from their discussion to bring about changes in behaviour. He had looked for information in the headaches he did have, and was able to pace himself so as to take some of the pressure off – much as the therapist had done. The therapist had 'modelled' to the client a resourceful approach to the problem symptoms, which the client had been able both to understand consciously and to use to inform himself and alleviate his symptoms. The first headache, he reported, had not returned even when the medication had worn off. The second, later in the week, had alerted him, prior to an important meeting with his manager, to clarify in his own mind what he wanted from the meeting, so that he was able to argue coherently and achieve at least some of the outcomes he wanted.

As the session drew to a close, Gerry commented: 'You know, this week was actually better than I realised. I'm beginning to think that I need to take the pressure off myself sometimes. It's not just what they're doing to me, what he's doing to me: it's also what I'm doing to myself.'

In NLP terms the *locus of control* was shifting back to the client. By the end of this session Gerry was beginning to be able to take a 'meta-position' in relation to his situation – to step outside it and to gain some useful distance from it. Once removed in this way, he was no longer so 'up against it', and could begin to assess his own role both in producing and in ameliorating the situation. He left feeling curious about how the following week would go, and how he would be able to manage any difficulties that arose.

Third session

Greeting Gerry on his return, the therapist observed that he looked both less tired and less twitchy. 'You're looking a lot better this week!' 'Yes . . .' replied Gerry, but in a tone of voice that implied some uncertainty. 'So . . .' said the therapist, matching the trailing off, 'What's the most useful thing we can do today?' After a longish pause, in which Gerry looked first up to his right, then down right, then down left (visual constructed → kinesthetic → internal dialogue), Gerry replied that he had intended talking more about how things were going at work; but that actually he would really rather talk about what was going on with Julia, his girlfriend.

He explained, rather hesitantly, that while they were very compatible in other ways, their sex life had been declining for some time. 'I'm always more enthusiastic at the beginning of a relationship – I know that – but then I tend to settle down into a rather low-key routine.' Julia's sex-drive had always been greater than his, and this had led to some tensions at times when Gerry was under pressure at work even while in the 'good' department. The change to the new job, together with the headaches, had affected him severely, and he had felt he had no energy for lovemaking. Even worse, because Julia's responses were easily triggered, he had begun avoiding ordinary non-sexual touching, fearing that it would arouse her expectations and lead to rows when he failed to respond.

Julia had made an effort to understand, and had apparently accepted that sleeplessness and headaches were the 'cause' of Gerry's diminished libido. However, since he had begun to sleep rather better, and in the last week had experienced only one, less severe, headache, she could not see why he was not as eager as she to resume lovemaking. It seemed, he said, that he had exchanged one source of stress for another: a better week at work had been cancelled out by a much worse one at home. He was beginning to fear that things would become even worse: if he could not regain his desire and perform more willingly, he could see Julia getting fed up and pulling out of the relationship. As a flight-attendant she met many people, crew and travellers: she was attractive and gregarious, and very physical. Why should she put up with him any longer? 'I can just see what's bound to happen. I go hot and cold thinking of it.'

The therapist recognised at the outset of the session that Gerry might be wanting to explore another area, and by matching his tone of uncertainty and asking him to specify the 'most useful' thing they could work on made it possible for Gerry to choose what he really wanted. The phrase 'most useful' is a presupposition (there are useful things to talk about – what is the *most useful of them*). Because it is non-specific, its meaning has to be supplied by the client; and in order to do this the client has to engage in an internal search to find what matches 'most useful' as far as they are concerned at this time. The process thus ensures that the client has the opportunity of selecting a topic which has considerable importance to them without the therapist in any way presupposing or determining what that might be.

In addition the therapist now had available, right at the beginning of the session, important information via Gerry's eye-accessing cues about the representational sequences he was running internally: in other words, the precise way in which he was constructing his experience. Asked to nominate the 'most useful' thing they could do today, Gerry first made a picture in his mind's eye (V^c), then checked out how it would feel (K) and then consulted with himself about it (A^id) before articulating his answer. A little later, the first steps in this sequence appeared again: 'I can just see what's bound to happen. I go hot and cold thinking about it.' Here the disaster scenario of Julia leaving him through frustration was visual (V^c), which led to feelings (K) of anxiety or panic. This session began to indicate that many of these overwhelming feelings might be triggered by 'bad' pictures.

As far as the relationship with Julia was concerned, the couple seemed to be stuck in a 'two-point loop' of repeating actions and reactions. His lower libido led to lowered sexual activity

- which led to her frustration;
- which in turn led to her becoming irritated and/or more demanding;
- which in turn led to Gerry avoiding most physical contact;
- which led to Julia's increased frustration.

While the tiredness and the headaches had temporarily given them some respite from this pattern, Gerry's improved health had now restored it again. The therapist noted, without remarking upon it to Gerry, that the headaches may have been serving another positive function for Gerry – they had been giving him an acceptable reason, in Julia's eyes, for being sexually distant.

The therapist asked Gerry how he knew that Julia loved him – what specific behaviours told him this? Gerry responded immediately that she used to tell him so quite frequently, though she now did this less often; and he had felt that her efforts to cook the kind of foods that would tempt his appetite had also shown that she was making an effort to support him. When the therapist asked what Gerry did that Julia thought showed his love for her, he replied unhesitatingly: 'Making love: that's what tells her I love her. That's why she's worried as well as angry at the moment. She thinks I must have stopped fancying her, and that's why I'm avoiding making love. She says she needs that from me.' 'And how do you think you show her you love her?' 'Well, by being there for her when she's wound up by something that happened at work; by doing the shopping and the cooking and the cleaning when she's away so that everything's all ready when she comes home; remembering her birthday – things like that. I never thought lovemaking was all that central – it's the icing on the cake, that's all.'

The therapist explained to Gerry that abstract concepts such as 'love' were always translated by people into specific behaviours which had meaning for them – and that though they might think that the word had the same meaning for their partner, it often did not. Because people were rarely specific to themselves or each other about what it did mean, there was plenty of room for ambiguity or misunderstanding. Gerry and Julia each had specific, but different, things in mind when they thought about loving or being loved: what NLP calls their 'criterial equivalences' for love did not match. In addition, it seemed that each had identified only a few behaviours. The therapist suggested that Gerry find a good moment to discuss this with Julia, so that each of them could identify other things which they felt expressed their love, and which on the other hand told them they were loved. In this way they would enrich their overall 'vocabulary', and build a shared understanding of what actions meant 'love' within their partnership.

The discussion of the relationship with Julia showed how Gerry was in a stuck or repeating loop at home, in addition to the pressures he was experiencing at work. The therapist introduced the concept of criterial equivalence and suggested the homework on it as a way of freeing the stuck pattern by helping the couple expand the range of activities which currently seemed to equate to love in their minds – and which had little overlap. By identifying and sharing a fuller range of specific behaviours that equated to 'love' they would be able to show each other their feelings more effectively, and also to take some of the pressure off the one specific behaviour, lovemaking, which had been taking most of the emphasis up till now. This might allow Julia to derive a sense of being loved in other ways, and Gerry to feel less of a failure – or at times less angry – for failing to perform. In fact, his unthinking use of the word 'perform' suggested that, for him, lovemaking had come to have a very different criterial equivalence – it was becoming a demand which he had to fulfill, not unlike the demands to 'fit in' at work.

Since Gerry was clearly distressed by the frequent disaster scenarios (V^c) of losing Julia, and felt little ability to reason himself (A^id) out of the bad feelings (K) they caused, the therapist showed him how he could freeze the movie at any point, and then shrink the single frozen frame down to the size of a full-stop. This process would allow him to hold the image unobtrusively until he had time to explore it further with the therapist, or to deal with it effectively in some other way himself. He did not need to run the whole movie. In addition, he could remind himself (A^id) that this was not yet happening, and might not have to happen. He asked Gerry to select a visual memory of a time in the past when he and Julia had been happy and relaxed together: Gerry remembered an incident on holiday in Italy, which he could see in bright, clear colours. With a little practise in the session, he found he could reduce the disaster movie to the size of a dot and then flood his mental 'screen' with a large, bright, cheerful image from the holiday – which in turn reactivated the good feelings that had gone with it.

Because Gerry's internal processing involved a clear sequence, the therapist was able to work with the different representational systems and the specific sub-modalities of those systems (colour, brightness, clarity, size) to help Gerry change his disaster patterning to a more productive one. The therapist also encouraged Gerry to remind himself (Id) that things could go differently – and to use this as a cue to re-access good experiences from the past. Gerry's representational sequencing ($V \rightarrow A^id \rightarrow K$) had been respected but modified. The disaster movie (V) had been modified, the internal dialogue now challenged the 'I just know how this will go' with a reminder that 'it doesn't have to be like that', leading to the retrieval of an encouraging and pleasant remembered picture (V^r), which in turn led to better feelings (K). Importantly, this modification of Gerry's processing went alongside showing him ways to help himself and his partner break out of their existing two-point loop and amplify their range of equivalences for love.

Gerry left at the end of the session feeling curious about the way he processed experience internally, and wondering how able he would be to use his new learnings in the 'real' situation outside the therapist's office. He was also looking forward to talking with Julia, and felt real hope that this discussion would shift things. As he said: 'I really hope it will improve things between us; but if we can't find more areas of overlap at least I'll know we've tried.'

Fourth session

Gerry returned after a two-week gap, necessitated by his absence at a work conference, full of excitement. He said he had lots to report and hardly knew where to begin.

He had found an opportunity for the discussion with Julia very soon after the last session, though he admitted the timing might have been better as she was quite tired after returning from a long flight. Nonetheless, she had responded well to being asked what things told her he loved her: just asking, she said, told her he really cared, because no one had ever asked her before and she felt he really wanted to know. This meant a lot. She confirmed that lovemaking was really the most important thing that told her she was loved, though she 'knew rationally' it didn't need to be like that. But she had never been without a partner since she was sixteen, and being valued sexually was tremendously important to her. It 'told her she was a woman, that she mattered'. She was surprised to discover that Gerry's homemaking activities (shopping, cooking, cleaning) were also messages of loving, and said that though she had always appreciated them, she hadn't realised before that they had this extra significance as far as he was concerned. He felt she was now much more aware of his love for her than she had been before, and that this had taken some of the pressure off lovemaking itself even though she still felt it was the single most important statement for her.

For himself, Gerry was unsure as to whether he had gained any information about other ways in which Julia's behaviour meant that she loved him. He felt that he was supposed to be reassured by the facts that she still desired him so much, and that she had rejected approaches from both colleagues and passengers at work.

However, he had been excited ever since the previous session by his new understanding of how his own mind was working: 'Sometimes it's as though there's a bit of me watching myself, and marvelling at the complexity of it – even when I'm getting in my own way', he said. A friend had phoned to ask him why he had been missing what used to be a regular session at the gym, and to suggest that they met for a game of squash, and Gerry had realised how much the joint pressures of work and home had been interfering with what had once been a busy social life. Before his promotion he had managed to find time to go to the gym a couple of times a week, and to play squash at least once; and he had enjoyed the friendships he made there, which had often spilled over into drinks or lunch at the pub afterwards.

'I started thinking about friendship', he explained, 'And I began to wonder how my friends would know I was still their friend, given how hermit-like I've been recently. I had turned this invitation down, because I really needed to finish writing a project proposal, but then I thought my friend would feel hurt and disappointed, since he'd bothered to phone me. I could see that if I went on like this much longer my friends would dwindle away, and before long I wouldn't have any. I had visions of dying a lonely old man. I frightened myself. So I shrank the picture, like we did last time, and reminded myself that it didn't have to be like that, and then I found another picture of a really good evening we all had after a tournament at the club, and made that clear and large and bright. After that I felt better – but I thought I'd better write my proposal some other time, even if it was rushed, and see if I could make the game after all. Luckily my friend hadn't given up on me, so we're meeting tomorrow. I feel as though I've escaped by the skin of my teeth.'

Gerry had been able to use what he had learnt in the session in a number of ways: he had opened up a discussion with Julia which had had some useful results, even though he had not felt as much benefit as she seemed to; he had generalised his learning unconsciously, so that although his first response to his friend's invitation was to say 'no' he had quickly found himself exploring the equivalent meanings 'friendship' had for him, and making new arrangements about his work so that he could show his continued commitment to his friends; he had also been able to repeat the modified representational system sequence when he began running the disaster scenario pattern, and had effectively changed how he felt as a result.

The therapist then asked 'What's it like now?', and Gerry replied that being able to step back from his immediate experience and observe its patterns had made him feel less stuck – he felt more adult and more resourceful – even though he had become aware of a problem that hadn't struck him before, the possible loss of friendships. Having recognised this and done something about it, he now felt he was at least in a position to make choices and think about managing the different demands on his time and energy. The problem, oddly enough, didn't seem bigger or more overwhelming even though he now recognised that it had more ramifications than he had at first thought. Following this up, the therapist said: 'And when you see how you're doing now, becoming aware that you do have choices as well as pressures, how do you feel?' Gerry replied that walking home the day before he had felt pleased with himself – almost as if he had grown taller. 'Definitely lighter in my step.' The therapist noted that as he said this, Gerry sat up straighter, and that his posture became more open.

T: You know what you don't want: you don't want to neglect your friendships because of overload at work and pressure at home. So what *do* you want in your future?

G: Well, I thought I would make a list of all the people I value, family and friends, and put it on the fridge door. Then when I get in and make myself a cup of tea after work, I can think about who I'd like to phone. I don't expect I'll have time every day, but even if I made two or three contacts a week I'd be really pleased. I'd feel I was doing something for me – something I *want* to do not just running to catch up with all the things I *ought* to do.

In this exchange, the therapist is modelling a movement from a problem frame towards an outcome frame, confirming and reinforcing Gerry's pride in himself and his sense that he now has more options, then gets him to 'future-pace' himself. In describing his list, and even where he plans to place it, Gerry is contextualising his desired outcome, giving it enough realism and detail to make it compelling. He has linked the idea of the list into his normal getting-home routine, which will tend to trigger the new behaviour. In so doing, he has actually also *reframed* the routine itself from its original meaning (switch-off i.e. *away-from*) to a new one (reward i.e. *towards*).

Fifth session

Gerry returned the following week reporting that his sleep patterns were virtually back to normal and that he had only had one headache since the last session. He was feeling much more in control, and had been able to phone two of his 'listed' friends. He had managed to fit in a game of squash as arranged and also one session at the gym. 'I wasn't going to push my luck by trying to fit in more than that,' he said. Things with Julia had been better, and he had been pleased to find himself actually wanting to make love for the first time in ages. They had decided to have a long weekend away together, taking advantage of a cheap last-minute flight she could get through her work on the airline. 'We don't quite know when it will be, but I've promised I'll rearrange things if I have to: we agreed it's really important that we have this time together soon.'

He had been disappointed to have a headache at all. 'I thought we'd cracked it, but I guess that was too much to expect.' He went on to explain that the headache had struck on a day he had set aside to prepare for an important meeting. 'I hadn't expected any problems because there was no pressure – in fact I'd told my secretary to take messages, and to tell people I would phone back the following day.' Nonetheless, by midmorning he was aware of the old feeling of compression building up. He tried to ignore it, but by lunch-time it had got really bad, just as it used to before commencing therapy. 'I thought, oh, it's back again just as bad as ever, and felt really disappointed. Then I thought, no, what's it telling you? What's it doing for you? Part of me wanted to crawl into a hole by this time, and part of me was determined to make full use of the time I'd cleared for myself. It felt like an impasse.'

The therapist asked: 'So what is each part achieving for you?'

Gerry thought for a moment, looking down left, then replied: 'Well, obviously the part that wanted to plough on with the preparation wanted to help me get the work done, be really ready with everything at my fingertips for the meeting, so I could answer any questions, deal with any challenges.'

'And the other part?'

'That part wanted to stop me putting so much pressure on myself. I think I was over-preparing, really, trying to be too perfect, get every option covered.'

'So both of them were really trying to help you.'

'Yes, I suppose so. But they were trying in such opposite ways: one part by covering all the options, the other by stopping me going mad with it. It was like an argument without words – really doing my head in . . . Oh . . . Listen to what I've just said!'

The therapist suggested that Gerry could ask the two parts to have a conversation with words, rather than an argument without them, since both were trying to achieve something important for him. 'You could do it now, just quietly in your head.'

Gerry became very still, looking into the distance, and remained so for several minutes. Then, refocusing on the therapist, he said that he had felt a sense of surprise that both parts were really aiming for the same thing: his well-being and indeed his effectiveness at work. As the internal conversation progressed, he had realised that he had a very stop–go approach to work: all or nothing; and that this wasn't really effective. The headaches had been trying all along to modify the overworking, but because he had tried to ignore them until they became really debilitating they had only resulted in him having to stop altogether. 'I need to explore the ground in the middle.'

The therapist said it sounded as if this was a familiar pattern to Gerry, and Gerry said it was. 'I think it's been going ever since I graduated, really. When I was a student I really enjoyed the life – friends, pubs, societies, and all that. Work had to fit in round the edges. I was so into it all that I couldn't see finals getting closer at all – then suddenly it was on top of me and I hadn't done enough. I got a degree, I know, but it wasn't anywhere near as good as I could have achieved if I'd put my mind to it. I vowed I'd never be shown up like that again: if I was going to do anything I'd do it properly, make sure I was really prepared. So I think that's what's got me feeling I'm always on the run, trying to catch up with myself. I've been a bit better at listening to myself since I've been coming here, but I really need to do something to end this push–pull kind of thing.'

The therapist asked Gerry to stand up, and to imagine a line on the floor connecting his past, through his present, to his future. Gerry found he immediately knew in which direction past and future were on the line, and stood beside the line looking rather puzzled but intrigued. The therapist then asked Gerry to step onto the line in the present, and walk slowly backwards until he reached 'the younger you who just lived to party, for whom finals was always miles away'. Gerry walked backwards for a few steps, hesitated and then stopped. He looked surprised, then said: 'How odd. It's like I'm not "just remembering" – it's more like I'm there: lots of times I'd quite forgotten . . . all the opportunities . . . but never quite having enough time to do the reading, or the projects . . . Somehow, they always get squeezed out.'

The therapist told Gerry to step off the time-line for a moment, and asked him what that younger self needed to help him then. Without hesitation, Gerry replied: 'He needs to be able to prioritise, to see what he needs to do as well as what he feels like doing and get it in some kind of proportion.'

The therapist then asked Gerry whereabouts in his life he did have the skill the younger self needed. 'Well, I'm beginning to get a grasp of that now. In spite of the hiccups, I'm better able to plan out my time and manage to do some of what I want in my private life, and not let my work take over – or be jeopardised either like it used to be.'

'OK. Then step onto the time-line in the present, facing that younger self, and let him know what prioritising involves and how to go about it.'

Gerry stepped onto the line, facing towards the past, and closed his eyes. As he stood there silent for a few moments, his head nodded slightly several times. Then he opened his eyes. 'I've done that. What next?'

'Step off the line again, then step back into that younger self and receive that information: really let in it sink in.'

As Gerry did so, he again closed his eyes, taking a big breath and letting it out heavily, blowing it out through his lips. Then he said: 'OK?'

'Yes. Now walk slowly forwards on the line until you reach the you that promised himself he'd never let himself be in that position again – he'd always be thoroughly prepared, and just take that understanding about prioritising, about the importance of having room for everything, with you, so that he can have it too.'

Gerry took a small step forward, then became still, first frowning then becoming more relaxed facially. His shoulders also dropped and he straightened and stood more upright. 'That feels much better. It's like a weight off me,' he said. 'I'm going to have to practise, but I know it can be done.'

'Yes. And now walk slowly forward up to the present, just letting that understanding inform all the times in-between. Stop for a moment anywhere you need to give yourself a chance for it to sink in . . .'

Gerry paused several times before reaching his 'present' position. 'It's amazing – it was like I was going through those years again, but seeing things quite differently. The events were all the same – but somehow the conflicts had gone out of them.'

'Now walk forward even further, into the future, knowing that you can listen to that inner voice, pay attention to what your body is telling you, and find the right weight to give to the different things you want and need to do . . . How is it, knowing that you have all these choices, so much more information available to you?' 'It's wonderful – such a relief. I'm really excited. I'm looking forward to it all.'

Gerry had taken active steps to manage the conflicting demands on his attention and time, and to set his priorities. But he had still experienced the conflict which went along with the headaches, recognising this time that it was like an argument between two parts of himself. The therapist reframed the conflict as one involving two positive intentions, and invited Gerry to explore both the aims which the two conflicting parts had and to ask them to engage in a negotiation, each recognising that their overall intent, Gerry's welfare, was a shared one. This experience allowed Gerry to remember how his experience of living for the moment as an undergraduate had resulted in him getting a poor degree – and how in turn he had made a self-limiting decision – never to be shown up like that again. Thus, the two sides of the repeating conflict were established: overdriving himself to achieve at work now activated a part which tried to protect him not by having fun, since he would have ignored it, but by creating physiological symptoms which he could not ignore. Working with the timeline allowed Gerry to physicalise his experience of time, and made it possible for him to change the way he had codified the past by integrating more recent resources into it.

It is significant that this procedure also provides for the transformation of events in-between, since in walking from the originally limiting but now transformed experience forward to the present, the client resources and recodifies intervening experiences which had once been limited also. Finally, the therapist had asked Gerry to future-pace himself by taking his new understandings forward into the future, experiencing the differences they will make with events yet to come.

This session was a very rich and eventful one, in which internal processing was strongly demonstrated by changes in Gerry's physiology. As he left, he said: 'Things are a lot clearer now – I'm beginning to feel there really is a way forward.'

Sixth session

Gerry began the session by telling the therapist that he felt this would probably be the last session. He had almost cancelled, but then realised that he wanted to let the therapist know in person how much he had learnt, and how much freer and more flexible he felt as a result of their work together. 'I'm surprised that it hasn't been a painful process,' he said, 'though we've certainly covered some topics that could have been. I've felt excited at times, and that I'd never have expected! I feel much more focused – more solid – now. I'm still under pressure, of course, at home, and at work, but when I hit a problem now I'm thinking *there must be a way round it.*'

He said that he was realising more and more strongly that he missed the inventiveness that had characterized his work in his old department, and that he was fairly clear that however much he worked on himself there would still be little room for this in the new one, partly because of his manager and partly because of the established culture of the rest of the team. 'I'm facing the fact that changing that isn't just going to take time – more like beating my head against a brick wall.'

The therapist asked him to see the future for a moment, and to discuss with himself how it felt if this was the case.

Gerry was quiet for a few moments, then responded:

G: Actually, I'm beginning to wonder whether I'm really suited to this job after all.

T: Or whether it's really suited to you . . .?

G: Yes, that's more like it, isn't it. I know I can do the job – but I also know what the costs are. I don't have to make myself fit in any more. I could start looking for other jobs, see whether I can find one that's more me. Friends have told me I could go freelance, be a consultant. It's always felt very risky; but I suppose I could think about that in detail, work out some costings, take it that bit further rather than just assuming it wouldn't work.

T: Yes. Let yourself see how it might be, then use that internal voice of yours to help you examine the pros and cons, and check out how it feels. That voice used to come up with all the doubts and problems – so it can be a resource when that's actually what you want to do. But this time you know how to have a conversation with it, a productive dialogue. If you hear the doubts and find ways round them, then you're really benefiting. And when you then ask yourself how that feels, you've added a kinesthetic check. So all three representational systems are involved and working for you.

Together they explored some of the possibilities Gerry was beginning to consider, and what impact they might have on his home life as well as on work. He was still not sure whether he and Julia would stay together long-term, or whether their needs and wishes, not just sexual ones, were too different. He was realising now, he said, that Julia's ever-changing lifestyle was not just a feature of her airline work but something which she really enjoyed. 'I'm more a homebody,' he said. 'I really want stability, and actually I don't really enjoy the feeling of change and excitement all that much in my private life. But I know that I want to explore all this with her, to be fair to both of us; and to do that, I've got to give us a chance. So that means being really firm about how much of my life I let work take over, and it means giving myself space to relax, on my own as well as when I'm with her.'

As the session came to a close, Gerry reflected on how he felt he had changed. 'When I came here,' he said, 'I just wanted a breathing space – a way to sleep better and to avoid those dreadful headaches. I couldn't see beyond that. Now I'm realising, not only why I was having those problems and how to get rid of them, but also that that's just the beginning. It's not just a weight off my chest to be able to expect one day to follow another without tossing and turning or that imprisoning pain – it's more like I can see possibilities for my life I wasn't even aware of before. It's sometimes a bit scary, but I'm feeling that I'm in charge now.'

In this final session Gerry was summing up the changes he had experienced in terms of an enlarged vision of life, not merely the removal of the symptoms that had brought him. His motivation had changed from an *away-from* to a *towards*; and he was feeling that he was now in charge of his life, even though two major issues – his job and the future of his relationship with Julia – still remained uncertain. The difference was one of locus of control: he was no longer feeling at the mercy of his new boss, of work overload, of Julia's greater libido, but feeling able to ask 'What do I want?' and know that he could find his own answers.

Ana

In phoning to make her appointment, Ana explained that she needed help for a forthcoming interview. She had passed a preliminary screening for a new post within her organisation, and had been chosen for a final short list. If successful, she would take up the new post very quickly and would be going abroad: it was therefore quite possible that she would only have time for one session. Because of this constraint, the therapist agreed to set aside between one and a half and two hours for the session. Her manner on the phone was calm, clear and efficient, her voice well-modulated, her vocabulary and syntax suggesting that she was well-educated.

Her appearance, when she arrived, was in keeping with this impression: she was wearing a dark grey, classic suit with a soft mulberry silk shirt, both complementing her Asian colouring.

> T: Hi, Ana, it's good to see you. You said on the phone that you had an important interview to prepare for, and that this was likely to be the only session we have, so can you tell me what you'd like us to achieve today?

A: That's right. I was thinking about how little time we had, and I thought it would be best to write things down so that I could tell you quickly what you need to know. I'm not sure, though, how much history you want?

T: Probably not a lot – now is where the opportunities are! But you're the expert on you, after all. So you're the best judge.

A: Oh – I hadn't thought of it like that. I don't feel like an expert – the reverse, in fact, when it comes to this situation! . . . Well, then . . . I'm 28, my parents came here from India, but I've never been there. I guess, though, I've got my hardworking ethic from them. Quiet, conscientious, keeping in the background, that's me. O levels, A levels, university – good solid grades. I had to work for it all: I'm not brilliant but I make the most of what I've got. I work late and get up early – just like helping mum and dad in our Post Office. OK. I got a job in a pharmaceutical company (my degree's in Chemistry), first of all in-house, then as a rep. I did well – I was asked to head up an area team. I can do it: I like people, I'm OK with my small team. I spend too much time preparing, probably, when I've got a meeting or a presentation – still, that's in my time.

T: So you've got a lot to feel good about?

A: Yes. I'm good at my job. I like it. I hadn't really thought any further ahead. Then one day, out of the blue really, my area manager called me in and said there was a bigger job going in the company: we're expanding into Europe, setting up an office in Brussels, they need a team leader to manage the reps there, and travel all over. He thought I should apply. It really surprised me. I hadn't thought I was that calibre at all.

T: You look like you were thrown by that, rather?

A: Yes, I was. It opened up possibilities I'd never considered – and it felt very scary. The one thing I've never liked doing is speaking in front of strangers. I forced myself to do it at university when I had to – hours of preparation, to make sure I had every possible question covered, sleepless nights, that kind of thing. Fortunately, as a scientist I didn't have to present all that often. But it's all coming up again now. I'm fine with my team – I know them. I'm fine with the customers – I've got the information or I know where to get it. I was OK at the first interview – the selectors were all people I knew and it was quite informal. How did I see my career developing, what were my strengths, what could I bring to this job – I'd been able to foresee all that. But this next interview is going to be different: the panel will all be strangers; it's being held at our Head Office, so I'm not familiar with the place; there'll be other candidates there and I know they'll be more confident than me; I've got to make a formal presentation, and I can just see myself faltering, drying up even. I'm already beginning to tense up, just thinking about it. Last night I dreamed about it: something went wrong with the OHP, I'd brought the wrong set of notes. I could see their faces getting contemptuous. It was so awful I woke myself up.

T: It looked pretty bad, then? And is that how you see it now?

A: Pretty much so. [Looks up right] Yes. It's not the same as the dream – nothing as obvious as the machinery going wrong, and I certainly won't take the wrong notes: that's not me. But I can see myself losing the thread, drying up, losing the subtler points which are the ones I really need to make. [Head and shoulders incline forwards; Ana looks down right]

T: And how does that feel? What are you noticing, right now?

A: Not good. My stomach feels tight – it's as though I'm hunching forward to protect it. And my shoulders are uncomfortable – tense right across. It's like when I did that presentation in my second year. I just want to be out of it. It's silly, isn't it. I'm only thinking about it, and it's already bad.

T: Not silly, no. Not at all. Is there anything else you notice?

A: Well, it's odd, but there's a bit of me that feels angry, too. I don't know what that's about – after all, it's my choice to be there. No one has made me do it. But I hate feeling so vulnerable – it's like I'm exposed or something. About to be found out. This doesn't make any sense – I know I can do the job. I know my manager has given me a good reference. I've got a good chance of it – I've been told that.

T: But it doesn't feel at all like that?

A: No, not at all. I could almost cry. I knew I needed help, but this is more than I expected.

T: OK. You know how important this is – that more is involved than you thought. And we can respect that. But let's just change focus for a moment. You're not like this every time you're presenting, or in a group, right?

A: No, not at all.

T: Tell me about some of the different times.

A: Well . . . [*Sits up, takes breath.*] Well, when I'm running our weekly team meeting, for example. [*Looks up left*] I know we haven't a lot of time, because they have to get out to their calls, but I want it to be a relaxed as well as purposeful time. So I make sure the meeting room is ready, there's coffee, biscuits, fruit juices. I make space for everyone to say how their last week has been and what they hope for this week. It's a mixture of checking back, reporting in, team building, goal setting. [*Looks horizontally left*] I know I do that well. Sometimes there's something new to introduce to them – I prepare that so it's clear and brief, so they can take it and run with it immediately. [*Voice is decisive, stronger. Looks down right.*]

T: And that feels . . .?

A: Very different! I'm confident. I enjoy it. I know I can do it.

T: And how do you know that?

A: Well, I'm reminding myself of all the times we've been together as a team, of how I built that team. Like we were a team at home in the Post Office: we had a couple of part-timers; we could all do everything, more or less, by the time I was doing my A levels, so it was just a question of seeing what needed to be done and working around each other. It had a kind of flow. That's how I like to think of my team now – on a good day we have that kind of confidence in each other.

T: So that's how you know your team in Europe could be . . .?

A: Yes – if I manage to get there!

T: OK. So you've got two very different scenarios here. One is anxious, tense, closed down – a bit angry, surprisingly, feeling you're becoming less fluent, less expansive, losing the thread. Your posture, your voice, both showing up how you feel. [*Therapist repeats Ana's accessing cues as she summarises verbally.*]

A: Yes.

T: And the other: you're confident, you're able to take charge, make things good and supportive for the others. Build a team where people can potentially work equally and effectively with each other. And as you go about it, your posture is open, relaxed, your voice is clear, calm, you're looking ahead . . . [*Therapist again models the dramatic change in physiology that went with Ana's description.*]

A: Yes.

T: And the difference is . . .?

A: Well, it's not just that in one I'm having to make a presentation, or that it's in front of strangers. I thought it was . . . but . . . [*Ana looks down right*]

T: But? . . . Take a moment, and just pay really close attention to these feelings . . .

[*Ana becomes still, looks up right, then down right. Frowns. Posture begins to incline forward and down. Lower lip trembles*]

T: That's right . . . . And just ride these feelings back into the past . . . right back to where they came from . . . That's right . . . All the way back to the very first time you felt like that . . .

A: Oh . . . I never realised . . . so that's it . . . [*Colour changes – neck becomes red – eyes moisten*]

T: OK . . . So you've just learnt something rather important about where those feelings come from, and you don't have to tell me unless you want to, because the person who needed to know was you.

A: No, I'd like to. It was when I was in my first GCSE year – O level maths. I was good at Maths up till then – never top, but always in the top ten in my class. I had to work at it, but I managed quite well. Our old teacher was really good – encouraging. Then she left, and we started the O level year with a new teacher. I suppose now that he was inexperienced, really, but he came across as very confident. We hadn't had many men teaching us before then: he was over six foot and quite burly – he used to tower above us as he walked round the desks. He used to set us problems to work out; I mostly got the right answers, though I didn't always know why or how . . . One day we were doing this, and he was asking different people what answers they'd got, and then working through the problem out loud to help people who'd got it wrong. And he picked on me. So I gave my answer – which was right. And he said how had I got there – explain my workings. And I couldn't. I don't remember if I really forgot, or if it was just being asked to explain in front of the whole class like that . . .

T: And when you couldn't . . .?

A: He was horrible. He said: 'And you're in the top set? You'll have to smarten your act up. Getting the right answer's useless if you can't demonstrate how you got there. If you go on like this you won't even be getting the right answers much longer. Stop wasting everyone's time. You might as well give up and work in Tesco's'. That's what started it all. That's how I feel when I think of the interview – small and stupid.

T: And angry?

A: Yes: he had no business to treat a child like that.

T: So now you know how you learnt to be scared of answering questions in front of people . . . And you also know how not to feel like that, don't you?

A: Yes. I do. But somehow I can't find a way to feel those feelings instead.

T: Just imagine in your mind's eye that you're looking at a movie screen – out there [*gestures to space in front of Ana*]. Yes?

A: Yes, I can see one.

T: OK. Now as you stay sitting here, run the movie of that experience, so that you can see that you back there . . . then . . . and ask yourself as you do, so now, I'm wondering, from the vantage point of now, what is the learning in that experience?

A: Well, I can see that it wasn't her fault at all: she did need to know how she got the answers she did, but that was absolutely the wrong way for him to approach it. He was incompetent – from where I sit he was probably even sexist – 'what can you expect from a girl?' – that kind of thing.

T: So as you watch that younger you, let her know in your own way that you're there for her, reaching out to her from her future . . .

A: Well, that's comforting . . . She's surprised I've got so far . . . Pleased . . .

T: And tell her how you now see that teacher, share your new perspective on him and how he behaved . . .

A: Yes! She's even angrier now. [*Sits really upright, squares shoulders*] She knew he wasn't nice, wasn't fair. But she didn't have any way of telling that she was right. She believes in herself more now.

T: Great. And take a moment now to run that movie forward, seeing how things can be been different afterwards with this new understanding. Fast-forward then, pause where you need to, just to let that new knowledge become part of her experience all the way up into your present . . . Notice how that makes things look and feel different . . .

[*Ana looks into the distance. Her face and posture go through several changes as she does this. There are several smiles. Then she refocuses and looks directly at the therapist.*]

A: Yes. It makes a real difference. I'm amazed. I didn't expect this at all. It's like a whole lot of things have become clearer. I don't feel so careful, so restricted, now.

T: That's great. Now let's look further ahead. But before we do that, I'd like you to notice what feeling less restricted, more believing in yourself, feels like. Where do you actually notice that?

A: In my body, do you mean?

T: Yes. Your body enacts, or holds, or expresses, or reflects, if you like, what you feel. You've noticed how it changes . . . Where and how are you experiencing these feelings of self-belief?

A: [*Pauses, defocuses, then looks down right*] Well, there's an uprightness in my shoulders – like they're wider apart. And my spine is taller somehow. And my head doesn't feel heavy. It's lighter now.

T: OK. Now really pay attention to these feelings. Do you notice anything else about them?

A: Yes, actually. That bit between my shoulder blades is warm – really cosy. And it's as though my neck isn't made of bone, just of air. Really floating.

T: Great. Now, keeping these feelings, let yourself think of some situation or other which is everyday or even boring.

A: Like washing up?

T: Yes, like that. How is that now?

A: [*Laughs*] Well, still a chore, but somehow a better kind of chore! As though it would just get itself done. Not a hassle.

T: Fine. And now just concentrate on the feelings again.

A: Yes.

T: OK. Now I want you to let those good feelings go – just for now.

A: All right – but I'd really rather keep them.

T: I know – and you can have them back again. [*Ana nods as she lets them go.*] Now just let them come back.

A: That's better!.

T: OK. Now think of something mildly difficult or frustrating where it would be really good to have those feelings available to you.

A: When I've got a really busy day and I have to rush from one place to another, where there's traffic and I'm not sure if I can keep to my appointments?

T: Yes. And keep those feelings with you as you rush through that day, just noticing now it's different.

A: [*Pauses, stares ahead with eyes defocused. A smile grows*] That's amazing . . . It's still a rush, but I feel better about it. I know that if I'm late it isn't my fault. I can just apologise, and explain about the traffic. I don't have to be so perfect.

T: And that's –

A: A relief.

T: OK – now let the feelings go again . . . Now get them back again . . . Now let them go again . . . Now get them back again.

A: It seems so easy.

T: It is easy, when you know how. And keeping the warmth, the floating, let yourself experience the day of your interview, from waking up in the morning right through to going to bed at night. You could play with different versions – familiar questions, unexpected questions; nice inter-viewers, more formal or even critical ones. You can run and stop and start and pause the video, just where you want to.

[*Several minutes of silence*]

A: [*Turns to therapist, smiling*] I wish I'd done this before – I could have saved myself so much anxiety! It was really interesting. I started with easy situations, then I got bolder and invented some difficult questions – I even had a brusque male manager a bit like the teacher!

T: That was bold of you!

A: Yes – but I reminded myself that his manner was his affair, and it didn't have to affect me: I know I can do that job . . . In fact, something strange occurred to me as I went through it.

T: Yes?

A: Well – it sounds ridiculous, but now that I know I can manage the interview, I'm beginning to wonder whether I really want that job after all.

T: Oh, really.

A: Yes – it's made me realise that I applied because I was told I should: I was flattered, it confirmed my feeling I could do something bigger – but it wasn't my own idea. Do you see what I mean?

T: Yes – you saw that you were – what? – doing what was expected of you? Doing the next thing?

A: Yes. That's what I've always done. O level, A level, university, job, pro-motion, now another promotion. Like a series of hurdles just coming up one after another. Wherever I've been in my life, I've just seen the next hurdle ahead. I've never really even wondered if I wanted to be there in the first place. I'm seeing it differently.

T: And now that you can look at it all from this different perspective, and wonder . . .?

A: I'm not sure. I'll have to think about that.

T: So one thing you could do, when you have a moment, is to run that video further ahead yet, and try out different scenarios. Test out how they look to you, how you feel about them. What would you be saying to yourself if you did this . . . or that . . .? That it was a good choice? Your choice? Or just a possibility that you chose not to take.

A: Yes . . . What I'm beginning to realise is that just because I *can* do something doesn't mean I *have* to. It's up to me.

T: Exactly.

A: One really odd thing: thinking about teaching, and how not to do it, makes me think I might like to have a try. I've enjoyed presenting new information to my team. I used to enjoy helping my brothers with their homework – they always said I was helpful. We seemed not to get into too many arguments, anyway. Maybe I should think about moving sideways in my company, find out about training?

T: Yes, you could certainly explore that. It's your choice. And how does having this wider set of possibilities make that interview seem to you now?

A: Well, I'll do the interview anyway, just for the practise. But now I shall sit there thinking *I certainly do want your interview, but you'll have to convince me that I want your job!*

T: That *is* a difference!

A: Yes, isn't it! I never thought I'd feel so in control!

Personal Postscript

If one approaches therapy from an integrational viewpoint, it becomes clear that many fields not labeled as 'human relations' disciplines had much to say about parts of the human gestalt long before human relations fields emerged. In my therapy and training, I make use of principles and ideas gleaned from the disciplines of dance, drama, religion, medicine, communications, education, speech, the behavioral sciences – even the physical sciences, from which the 'systems concept' (on which my practice is based) first derived. Integration, in theory and practice, of all the tools available to man for his growth is necessary before we begin to deal in fact with the 'total man'.

(Satir, *On Becoming a Person*, 1967: 179)

In Chapter 7 we stressed that therapists have as much right to benefit from the therapy they practice as their clients, and that our continued personal growth and development are an important – even when unarticulated – resource for them as well as for ourselves. That is our belief – and it is also our experience. As we were thinking about this, and about what we hope you have gained from reading the book you are now holding, we each became curious about how the other had become involved with NLP, and what they had gained from it.

Towards the end of the 1970s, Ian was very aware of how therapies tended to become insulated from one another, each with their beliefs, methodologies and clinical groupings. With a long-standing interest in looking for commonalities within the field, he deliberately chose for his own therapeutic training one which offered an eclectic approach, exploring the validity and strength of many different approaches. At this time, the first books on NLP, modelling the structure of excellent practice, were starting to be published. Ian's later training exemplified for him how very different approaches can be outstanding: at the same time as he undertook a training in NLP he also took the introductory year at the Institute of Group Analysis – both outstanding, both stimulating, yet very different.

As a student, then tutor, of English Literature, Wendy was also drawn to patterns, especially those of metaphor and the structure of language. Moving into group-work and the training of teachers took this awareness into practical applications within the interaction between dyads and groups, further emphasised in her training as a psychotherapist and hypnotherapist. At this point, she also encountered the early books on NLP, which though not studied on the course were personally recommended by a course tutor – and which she found far more fascinating and useful than the 'official' reading list!

We first met on a professional workshop not long after this, at about the time Ian was founding International Teaching Seminars (ITS) and Wendy was launching out into private practice and beginning to teach hypnosis and psychotherapy. Then there was a gap of about ten years, during which time Wendy often thought of taking an NLP training, but never felt justified in spending the time or the money 'on herself' when she could already 'do' many of the techniques.

During all this time, she remained on the ITS mailing list, and when planning a book with another colleague, decided to attend one of Ian's open evenings, entitled 'Constructing Your Future'. When Ian asked for examples of the kind of future people wanted to create, Wendy and her colleague said they wanted to write a book. They asked for tips in starting and one of the things Ian said was: 'What is important is to think about who will be wanting to read this book 18 months from now – and then write it for them.' And that is what Wendy and her colleague Jan did. Using this approach they wrote an outline and sample chapter of their book and found a publisher who commissioned them to write the rest. Prompted by the success of this approach, they both decided to take a training with ITS. It proved life-transforming in many ways, rather than an indulgence, and above all an in-the-muscle experience, where before the knowledge had been largely conceptual.

The writing of this book has thus been the most recent in a series of spontaneous and significant meetings. We invite you in turn to consider the chain of events which has led you to reading it. How come you were interested at this time? What does this tell you about what's important to you?

For both of us, discovering NLP and exploring what it has to offer us and our clients has been – and continues to be – an enabling, fascinating, exciting, and joyful experience. Our hope is that NLP may enrich not only your clients' experience but yours too.

Resources and Training

If you have found this book of interest you will benefit tremendously from actually experiencing good NLP training. Because NLP is skill-based you can learn a lot in a hands-on training programme that gives you the opportunity to test and try out the techniques, the how-to's and, above all, this way of thinking.

International Teaching Seminars is a world leader in quality NLP training. It also has links with many other NLP organisations around the world.

You can get further information via the web, by phone or fax or by mail:

Web: www.itsnlp.com
Phone: from inside the UK: 0207 247 0252
         from outside the UK: +44 207 247 0252
Fax: from inside the UK: 0207 247 0242
         from outside the UK: +44 207 247 0242
Mail: International Teaching Seminars
         19 Widegate Street
         London E1 7HP
         United Kingdom

Further NLP Presuppositions

In relation to the other chapter topics we have covered, the following NLP presuppositions are particularly useful:

Change

- People respond to their map of reality, but not to reality itself. NLP is the art of changing these maps, not changing the reality.
- It is easier to change yourself than others.

Presuppositions

- People already have all the resources they need – including those necessary to make any desired change.
- People work perfectly – no one is wrong or broken.

Modelling

- Modelling excellence leads to excellence.
- If one person can do something, it is possible to model it and teach it to others.

Mind–Body

- Mind and body are one integrated system.
- Communication is both verbal and non-verbal, both conscious and unconscious.

Client–Therapist System

- Rapport is meeting individuals at their map of the world.
- There are no resistant clients, only inflexible communicators.

Benefits to Client

- Every experience can be utilised.
- You are not your behaviour.

Benefits to Therapist

- Behaviour is the highest quality information.
- Individuals with the most flexibility have the highest probability of achieving the responses they desire.

References and Further Reading

Andreas, Steve and Andreas, Connirae (1987) *Change Your Mind, and Keep the Change*. Moab, UT: Real People Press.

Andreas, Steve and Andreas, Connirae (1989) *Heart of the Mind*. Moab, UT: Real People Press.

Ansbacher, Heinz L. and Ansbacher, Rowena R. (ed.) (1958) *The Individual Psychology of Alfred Adler*. London: Allen and Unwin.

Bandler, Richard and Grinder, John (1975) *The Structure of Magic, Volume One*. Palo Alto, CA: Science and Behavior Books.

Bandler, Richard and Grinder, John (1976) *The Structure of Magic, Volume Two*. Palo Alto, CA: Science and Behavior Books.

Berne, Eric (1969) *Games People Play*. Harmondsworth: Penguin.

Chopra, Deepak (1990) *Quantum Healing*. New York: Bantam Books.

Dilts, Robert (1990) *Changing Belief Systems with NLP*. Capitola, CA: Meta Publications.

Dilts, Robert and DeLozier, Judith (2000) *Encyclopedia of Systematic Neuro-Linguistic Programming*. Scotts Valley, CA: NLP University Press.

Dilts, Robert, Halbron, Tim and Smith, Suzi (1990) *Beliefs: Pathways to Health and Well-Being*. Portland, OR: Metamorphous Press.

Edwards, Monica (1952) *Hidden in a Dream*. London: Collins (1966 edition).

Erikson, Milton H. (1954) 'Pseudo-Orientation in Time as a Hypnotherapeutic Procedure' in Ernest L. Rossi (ed.) (1980) *Collected Papers, Volume IV*. New York: Irvington.

Goffman, Erving (1963) *Stigma: Notes on the Management of Spoiled Identity*. Harmondsworth: Penguin (1968 edition).

Gordon, David (1978) *Therapeutic Metaphors: Helping Others through the Looking Glass*. Capitola, CA: Meta Publications.

Lankton, Steve (1980) *Practical Magic: A Translation of Basic NLP into Clinical Psychotherapy*. Capitola, CA: Meta Publications.

Maslow, Abraham (1968) *Toward a Psychology of Being*. Princeton, NJ: Van Nostrand Co.

McDermott, Ian and O'Connor, Joseph (1996) *NLP and Health*. London: Thorsons.

McDermott, Ian and Shircore, Ian (1999) *Manage Yourself, Manage Your Life*. London: Piatkus Books.

O'Connor, Joseph and McDermott, Ian (2001) *Way of NLP*. London: Thorsons.

O'Connor, Joseph and McDermott, Ian (1997) *The Art of Systems Thinking*. London: Thorsons.

Remen, Rachel Naomi (1989) 'The search for healing', in R. Carlson and B. Shield (eds), *Healers on Healing*. Los Angeles, CA: Tarcher. p. 93.

Rogers, Carl Ransom (1967) *On Becoming a Person*. London: Constable & Co.

Rosen, Sidney (ed.) (1982) *My Voice Will Go With You: The Teaching Tales of Milton H. Erickson*. London: W.W. Norton.

Rossi, Ernest L. (1986) *The Psychobiology of Mind–Body Healing*. London: W.W. Norton

Shazer, Steve de (1988) *Clues, Investigating Solutions in Brief Therapy*. London: W.W. Norton.

Zeig, Jeffrey K. and Gilligan, Stephen G. (1990) *Brief Therapy*. New York: Brunner/ Mazel.

Index